I0758716

TENNESSEE PETITIONERS, ETC. AND GRAINGER COUNTY TAX LISTS 1800 [1795-1804]

Copyright 24 February 2021
Stemmons Publishing
1078 Shields Lane
South Jordan, Utah 84095

BIBLIOGRAPHY FOR

**TENNESSEE PETITIONERS, ETC. AND GRAINGER COUNTY TAX LISTS 1800
[1795-1804]**

United States, Department of State, compiled and edited by Clarence Edwin Carter, *The Territorial Papers of the United States* Washington, D.C.: Government Printing Office, 1934-1962. 26 volumes. National Archives microfilm publications: M0721
> vol. 1. The Territorial Papers of the United States, General.
> vols. II & III The Territory Northwest of the River Ohio, 1787-1803.
> vol. IV The Territory South of the River Ohio, 1790-1796.
> vols. V & VI The Territory of Mississippi, 1798-1817.
> vols. VII & VIII The Territory of Indiana, 1800-1816.
> vol. IX The Territory of Orleans, 1803-1812.
> vols. X - XII The Territory of Michigan, 1805-1837.
> vols. XIII - XV The Territory of Louisiana-Missouri, 1803-1821.
> vols. XVI & XVII The Territory of Illinois, 1809-1818.
> vol. XVIII The Territory of Alabama, 1817-1819.
> vols. XIX - XXI The Territory of Arkansas, 1819-1836.
> vols. XXII - XXVI The Territory of Florida, 1821-1845.

[Please note: *Larger lists of names, such as petitions, etc., will be entered into the database. Names found in regular governmental/public transactions that contain no individual biographical details will not be extracted.*]

TN-01 TENNESSEE PETITIONERS, ETC. AND GRAINGER COUNTY TAX LISTS 1800 [1795-1804] Also known as Territory South of Ohio River. This book was assembled from Grainger County Tax Lists 1800 and *Territorial Papers of the United States* and contains 182 names for the *Papers* and 247 names for the tax lists. From *Territorial Papers of the United States* the names mostly seem to be persons appointed to official or military positions or are members of the Knoxville Convention. Thus, they seem to be the more prominent persons, so, most of the less noteworthy individuals would not be listed. Still, the people listed clarify this early time before Tennessee became a state. The tax lists record the names of those who are taxable and are much more inclusive. They do include important details about the property they held. For information on how to obtain this book search by the title or "Books by John Stemmons" at Amazon.com. This comes automatically with a paperback binding. It includes but is not limited to petitions regarding:
- List, 21 Dec 1795, of members of Knoxville Convention.
- Appointments of military and local officers, etc.

INDEXES

Indexes are expensive to compile.

Which is why many books do not have them. Most that do just have a simple name index. A noteworthy exception is the *Territorial Papers of the United States* which gives some limited context as explained below.

Indexes are expensive but using modern technology we at Stemmons Publishing have included nearly all the context you may need. 100% context is probably not possible such as in a census that lists multiple neighbors. Search for entries of the same page in our book(s) or the original document if you require more information.

PUBLICATIONS FROM STEMMONS PUBLISHING

These following publications are not just traditional alphabetical lists of names, they include the context of information with each name!!

Why is that so important? Because many of the names in our books were obtained from various sources including South Carolina jury lists, the *Territorial Papers of the United States* (28 volumes each with its own index), petitions, tax lists, etc., and like most books with indexes common names require a lot of time to check each entry in the index. Can you imagine how many Smiths you would have to go through page-by-page for a compilation the size of *Territorial Papers of the United States*? Their indexes provide some context such as signing a petition. No explanation is given of what, when, or why the petition was made. Because we have included the context with each name, you can easily search all the Smiths, Taylors, Browns, Williams, etc., without all the drudgery! And since most of us have common surnames, we may need some help. Now, the originals of the South Carolina jury lists are housed in the South Carolina Department of Archives and History. Therefore, you may not have access to the originals. The way we index names means it is almost as good as being at the Archives yourself and doubly so since these documents are loose papers and do not have an original index. Our books provide an enhanced way of using *Territorial Papers of the United States* that the original compilers did not envision. So, if you have this collection, your obtaining our books compiled from those volumes will help your access to *Territorial Papers of the United States* even if you are not interested in our books about South Carolina jury lists. Now, that's what I call achieving the potential of a real index! It takes the bare skeleton of a name on a list and covers it with the flesh, hair, eyes, etc., of a human body. The names are more able to stand alone by themselves than is the case with a traditional index. We did not index subjects. *Territorial Papers of the United States* did.

Checking a name from our books and going to the page in *Territorial Papers of the United States* will show the list of names. Those listed next to the person of interest may be neighbors and relatives.

Guidelines for Entry of Names

Many times, names have been difficult to decipher. Other times, the document itself has been damaged in various ways that impacted our ability to read the information. Several methods have been employed to indicate to the reader when we had difficulty. They are as follows:

When a surname has been difficult to determine and could be read alternately, we have indicated this by using two and sometimes three possibilities. For example, Rud or Ried. For your convenience we have made separate entries for each possibility: Rud or Ried and Ried or Rud. We encourage individuals to go to the original source and make a determination for themselves if the name is important for their research. For given names, we will also indicate more than one possibility, but will not make separate entries for each one.

When an undetermined number of letters were unreadable, we used the ellipsis ". . ." in place of the letters we could not decipher, while we included those characters we could read. For example: Cr . . . [surname] and . . . seph [given name]. It would be difficult to determine the surname with confidence, but the given name is most likely "Joseph".

When a known number of characters could not be read, an asterisk "*" was used in place of each letter we could not decipher. Often the name can be determined based on where the asterisk is placed. For example, with Brow* one can readily determine the name is most likely Brown. However, when one or more asterisks are placed at the beginning of a name, the possibilities become more numerous and therefore difficult to determine.

When we were unsure about the reading, we would include a question mark "?" after the name.

Sometimes we could not read the name because the writing was too faint, it was covered with ink blotches, portions of the document was damaged/missing, or for many other reasons. We tried to indicate this when we felt a name was there by using "[Unreadable]", "[Missing]", "[Illegible]", "[Name crossed out]", etc., in place of the name. In some cases, a name might be read by examining carefully the original document.

When the first letter was obviously wrong and would interfere in a researcher's ability to readily see the name, we have placed in brackets what we thought the name should be along with the spelling of the name in the original. One can use the search feature on the Internet to find these names. An example is Knewkurk [Newkirk], Richard. A researcher might never know to look under the spelling Knewkurk and therefore miss potentially vital information. By searching for the name Newkirk, one would find this entry.

Sometimes it is difficult to tell which is the given name and which is the surname. When there has been doubt about the proper order of given name/surname, we have made an entry such as: Everet or Jones, [surname], and Jones or Everet [given name]. Then we have made another entry with the names reversed such as Jones or Everet [surname], and Everet or Jones [given name].

When deciphering entries, we have always tried to err on the side of reasonable, known, practical, and possible names rather than unreasonable, impossible, or impractical spellings.

TENNESSEE PETITIONERS, ETC. AND GRAINGER COUNTY TAX LISTS 1800
[1795-1804]

429 Names

***armer?, William?,** Tennessee, Grainger County
    *armer?, William?, Male
List of taxable property "Capt Margraves Compt 1799"; Lands: 0; "W[hite?] Poles": 1; "B[lack?] Poles": 0; "S[tud?] horses": 0; "Town Lots": 0.
Tennessee Records of Grainger County-Tax Lists, 1799, [TN State Library and Archives] FAMILY HISTORY LIBRARY film 464105
[Unreadable], [Unreadable], Tennessee, Grainger County
    [Unreadable], [Unreadable], Male
"Tax List Capt Jenings District taken in by Wm Hancock. 1797"; "W[hites?]": 0; "B[lacks?]": 0; "L[and?]": 0; "S[tud?] H[orses?]": 0.
Tennessee Records of Grainger County-Tax Lists, 1797 [TN State Library and Archives] FAMILY HISTORY LIBRARY film 464105
[Unreadable], [Unreadable], Tennessee, Grainger County
    [Unreadable], [Unreadable], Male
"List of Taxable Property Harris Company Taken by James Moore. 1798"; Land: 200; "W[hite?] Pole": 1; "B[lack?] Pole": 0; "S[tud?] Horse": 0.
Tennessee Records of Grainger County-Tax Lists, 1798, [TN State Library and Archives] FAMILY HISTORY LIBRARY film 464105
[Unreadable], [Unreadable], Tennessee, Grainger County
    [Unreadable], [Unreadable], Male
"Tax List Capt Jenings District taken in by Wm Hancock. 1797"; "W[hites?]": 0; "B[lacks?]": 0; "L[and?]": 0; "S[tud?] H[orses?]": 0.
Tennessee Records of Grainger County-Tax Lists, 1797 [TN State Library and Archives] FAMILY HISTORY LIBRARY film 464105
[Unreadable], [Unreadable], Tennessee, Grainger County
    [Unreadable], [Unreadable], Male

List of taxable property "Capt Margraves Compt 1799"; Lands: 0; "W[hite?] Poles": 1; "B[lack?] Poles": 0; "S[tud?] horses": 0; "Town Lots": 0.
Tennessee Records of Grainger County-Tax Lists, 1799, [TN State Library and Archives] FAMILY HISTORY LIBRARY film 464105
[Unreadable], [Unreadable], Tennessee, Grainger County
    [Unreadable], [Unreadable], Male
"Tax List Capt Jenings District taken in by Wm Hancock. 1797"; "W[hites?]": 0; "B[lacks?]": 0; "L[and?]": 0; "S[tud?] H[orses?]": 0.
Tennessee Records of Grainger County-Tax Lists, 1797 [TN State Library and Archives] FAMILY HISTORY LIBRARY film 464105
[Unreadable], [Unreadable], Tennessee, Grainger County
    [Unreadable], [Unreadable], Male
"Tax List Capt Jenings District taken in by Wm Hancock. 1797"; "W[hites?]": 0; "B[lacks?]": 0; "L[and?]": 0; "S[tud?] H[orses?]": 0.
Tennessee Records of Grainger County-Tax Lists, 1797 [TN State Library and Archives] FAMILY HISTORY LIBRARY film 464105
[Unreadable], Ed . . .?, Tennessee, Grainger County
    [Unreadable], Ed . . .?, Male
"List of Taxable Property Harris Company Taken by James Moore. 1798"; Land: ?; "W[hite?] Pole": ?; "B[lack?] Pole": 0; "S[tud?] Horse": 0.
Tennessee Records of Grainger County-Tax Lists, 1798, [TN State Library and Archives] FAMILY HISTORY LIBRARY film 464105
Acuf, John, Jr Tennessee, Grainger County
    Acuf, John, Jr Male
"Tax List Capt Jenings District taken in by Wm Hancock. 1797"; "W[hites?]": 1; "B[lacks?]": 0; "L[and?]": 0; "S[tud?] H[orses?]": 0.
Tennessee Records of Grainger County-Tax Lists, 1797 [TN State Library and Archives] FAMILY HISTORY LIBRARY film 464105

Acuf?, J . . .,   Tennessee, Grainger County
Acuf?, J . . .,   Male
"Tax List Capt Jenings District taken in by Wm Hancock. 1797"; "W[hites?]": 1; "B[lacks?]": 0; "L[and?]": 0; "S[tud?] H[orses?]": 0.
Tennessee Records of Grainger County-Tax Lists, 1797 [TN State Library and Archives]   FAMILY HISTORY LIBRARY film 464105

Adair, John,   Territory South of Ohio River, Knox County
Adair, John,   Male
List, 21 Dec 1795, of members of Knoxville Convention.
Territorial Papers of the US - volume: 4 page: 415

Adams, John,   Territory South of Ohio River, Washington County
Adams, John,   Male
On 11 Jul 1795 he was made a Justice of the Peace for Washington County.
Territorial Papers of the US - volume: 4 page: 468

Alexander, Jesse,   Territory South of Ohio River, Jefferson County
Alexander, Jesse,   Male
On 8 Jul 1795 he was made an Ensign in the Regiment of Infantry for Jefferson County.
Territorial Papers of the US - volume: 4 page: 468

Alexander, John,   Territory South of Ohio River, Blount County
Alexander, John,   Male
On 3 Aug 1795 he was made Cornet in the Cavalry for Blount County.
Territorial Papers of the US - volume: 4 page: 469

Alsup, Cain,   Tennessee, Grainger County
Alsup, Cain,   Male
"Tax List Capt Jenings District taken in by Wm Hancock. 1797"; "W[hites?]": 2; "B[lacks?]": 0; "L[and?]": 200; "S[tud?] H[orses?]": 0.
Tennessee Records of Grainger County-Tax Lists, 1797 [TN State Library and Archives]   FAMILY HISTORY LIBRARY film 464105

Alsup, James,   Tennessee, Grainger County
Alsup, James,   Male
"List of Taxable Property Harris Company Taken by James Moore. 1798"; Land: 235; "W[hite?] Pole": 1; "B[lack?] Pole": 0; "S[tud?] Horse": 0.
Tennessee Records of Grainger County-Tax Lists, 1798, [TN State Library and Archives]   FAMILY HISTORY LIBRARY film 464105

Anderson, John,   Tennessee, Grainger County
Anderson, John,   Male
List of taxable property "Capt Margraves Compt 1799"; Lands: 476; "W[hite?] Poles": 0; "B[lack?] Poles": 0; "S[tud?] horses": 0; "Town Lots": 0.
Tennessee Records of Grainger County-Tax Lists, 1799, [TN State Library and Archives]   FAMILY HISTORY LIBRARY film 464105

Anderson, Joseph,   Territory South of Ohio River, Jefferson County
Anderson, Joseph,   Male
List, 21 Dec 1795, of members of Knoxville Convention.
Territorial Papers of the US - volume: 4 page: 415

Archer, Curnilius,   Tennessee, Grainger County
Archer, Curnilius,   Male
List of taxable property "Capt Margraves Compt 1799"; Lands: 50; "W[hite?] Poles": 1; "B[lack?] Poles": 0; "S[tud?] horses": 0; "Town Lots": 0.
Tennessee Records of Grainger County-Tax Lists, 1799, [TN State Library and Archives]   FAMILY HISTORY LIBRARY film 464105

Armstrong, Robert,   Territory South of Ohio River, Knox County
Armstrong, Robert,   Male
On 26 Nov 1795 he was made an Ensign in the Knox Regiment.
Territorial Papers of the US - volume: 4 page: 470

Arnel, Wm,   Tennessee, Grainger County
Arnel, Wm,   Male
"List of Taxable Property Harris Company Taken by James Moore. 1798"; Land: 400; "W[hite?] Pole": 1; "B[lack?] Pole": 1; "S[tud?] Horse": 0.
Tennessee Records of Grainger County-Tax Lists, 1798, [TN State Library and Archives]   FAMILY HISTORY LIBRARY film 464105

Arnet, Jacob,   Tennessee, Grainger County
Arnet, Jacob,   Male
"List of Taxable Property Harris Company Taken by James Moore. 1798"; Land: 600; "W[hite?] Pole": 1; "B[lack?] Pole": 0; "S[tud?] Horse": 0.
Tennessee Records of Grainger County-Tax Lists, 1798, [TN State Library and Archives]   FAMILY HISTORY LIBRARY film 464105

Arwine, James,   Tennessee, Grainger County
Arwine, James, Male
"Tax List Capt Jenings District taken in by Wm Hancock. 1797"; "W[hites?]": 1; "B[lacks?]": 0; "L[and?]": 200; "S[tud?] H[orses?]": 0.

Tennessee Records of Grainger County-Tax Lists, 1797 [TN State Library and Archives] FAMILY HISTORY LIBRARY film 464105

arwine, John, Tennessee, Grainger County

arwine, John,   Male

"Tax List Capt Jenings District taken in by Wm Hancock. 1797"; "W[hites?]": 1; "B[lacks?]": 0; "L[and?]": 200; "S[tud?] H[orses?]": 0.

Tennessee Records of Grainger County-Tax Lists, 1797 [TN State Library and Archives] FAMILY HISTORY LIBRARY film 464105

Ashburn, Martin,   Tennessee,   Grainger County

Ashburn, Martin,   Male

"List of Taxable Property Harris Company Taken by James Moore. 1798"; Land: 600; "W[hite?] Pole": 0; "B[lack?] Pole": 0; "S[tud?] Horse": 0.

Tennessee Records of Grainger County-Tax Lists, 1798, [TN State Library and Archives] FAMILY HISTORY LIBRARY film 464105

Asher, David, Tennessee, Grainger County

Asher, David,   Male

"Tax List Capt Jenings District taken in by Wm Hancock. 1797"; "W[hites?]": 1; "B[lacks?]": 0; "L[and?]": 0; "S[tud?] H[orses?]": 0.

Tennessee Records of Grainger County-Tax Lists, 1797 [TN State Library and Archives] FAMILY HISTORY LIBRARY film 464105

Asher, David, Tennessee, Grainger County

Asher, David,   Male

His name is written vertically in the bottom center of the page.

"List of Taxable Property Harris Company Taken by James Moore. 1798"; Land: 0; "W[hite?] Pole": 0; "B[lack?] Pole": 0; "S[tud?] Horse": 0.

Tennessee Records of Grainger County-Tax Lists, 1798, [TN State Library and Archives] FAMILY HISTORY LIBRARY film 464105

Asher, William,   Tennessee,   Grainger County

Asher, William,   Male

List of taxable property "Capt Margraves Compt 1799"; Lands: 100; "W[hite?] Poles": 1; "B[lack?] Poles": 0; "S[tud?] horses": 0; "Town Lots": 0.

Tennessee Records of Grainger County-Tax Lists, 1799, [TN State Library and Archives] FAMILY HISTORY LIBRARY film 464105

Ashley, Noah, Tennessee, Grainger County

Ashley, Noah,   Male

List of taxable property "Capt Margraves Compt 1799"; Lands: 50; "W[hite?] Poles": 1; "B[lack?] Poles": "1 $150"; "S[tud?] horses": 0; "Town Lots": 0.

Tennessee Records of Grainger County-Tax Lists, 1799, [TN State Library and Archives] FAMILY HISTORY LIBRARY film 464105

Baker, George,   Tennessee,   Grainger County

Baker, George, Male

"List of Taxable Property Harris Company Taken by James Moore. 1798"; Land: 250; "W[hite?] Pole": 1; "B[lack?] Pole": 0; "S[tud?] Horse": 0.

Tennessee Records of Grainger County-Tax Lists, 1798, [TN State Library and Archives] FAMILY HISTORY LIBRARY film 464105

Basel, Thomas,   Tennessee,   Grainger County

Basel, Thomas, Male

"List of Taxable Property Harris Company Taken by James Moore. 1798"; Land: 0; "W[hite?] Pole": 1; "B[lack?] Pole": 0; "S[tud?] Horse": 0.

Page 33 is out of order and can be found on the microfilm following page 202. Page 33 has no heading, but the columns appear to be the same as those on page 32 and so will be considered as a part of that series. The entries appear to be crossed out.

Tennessee Records of Grainger County-Tax Lists, 1798, [TN State Library and Archives] FAMILY HISTORY LIBRARY film 464105

Bealor, Daniel,   Tennessee,   Grainger County

Bealor, Daniel, Male

"Tax List Capt Jenings District taken in by Wm Hancock. 1797"; "W[hites?]": 1; "B[lacks?]": 0; "L[and?]": 3**; "S[tud?] H[orses?]": 0.

Tennessee Records of Grainger County-Tax Lists, 1797 [TN State Library and Archives] FAMILY HISTORY LIBRARY film 464105

Bealor, John, Tennessee, Grainger County

Bealor, John,   Male

"Tax List Capt Jenings District taken in by Wm Hancock. 1797"; "W[hites?]": 0; "B[lacks?]": 1; "L[and?]": 240; "S[tud?] H[orses?]": 0.

Tennessee Records of Grainger County-Tax Lists, 1797 [TN State Library and Archives] FAMILY HISTORY LIBRARY film 464105

Bean, John, Tennessee, Grainger County

Bean, John,   Male

"Tax List Capt Jenings District taken in by Wm Hancock. 1797"; "W[hites?]": 1; "B[lacks?]": 0; "L[and?]": 1000; "S[tud?] H[orses?]": 0.
Tennessee Records of Grainger County-Tax Lists, 1797 [TN State Library and Archives] FAMILY HISTORY LIBRARY film 464105
Beard, Joseph, Tennessee, Grainger County
        Beard, Joseph, Male
"List of Taxable Property Harris Company Taken by James Moore. 1798"; Land: 550; "W[hite?] Pole": 0; "B[lack?] Pole": 0; "S[tud?] Horse": 0.
Tennessee Records of Grainger County-Tax Lists, 1798, [TN State Library and Archives] FAMILY HISTORY LIBRARY film 464105
Beelor, Joseph, Tennessee, Grainger County
        Beelor, Joseph, Male
"Tax List Capt Jenings District taken in by Wm Hancock. 1797"; "W[hites?]": 1; "B[lacks?]": 0; "L[and?]": 70; "S[tud?] H[orses?]": 0.
Tennessee Records of Grainger County-Tax Lists, 1797 [TN State Library and Archives] FAMILY HISTORY LIBRARY film 464105
Been, Stephen, Tennessee, Grainger County
        Been, Stephen, Male
"Tax List Capt Jenings District taken in by Wm Hancock. 1797"; "W[hites?]": 1; "B[lacks?]": 0; "L[and?]": 200; "S[tud?] H[orses?]": 0.
Tennessee Records of Grainger County-Tax Lists, 1797 [TN State Library and Archives] FAMILY HISTORY LIBRARY film 464105
Berry, Thomas, Territory South of Ohio River, Hawkins County
        Berry, Thomas, Male
On 2 May 1795 he was appointed Sheriff for Hawkins County.
Territorial Papers of the US - volume: 4 page: 467
Berry, Thomas, Territory South of Ohio River, Hawkins County
        Berry, Thomas, Male
On 27 Jan 1796 he was designated Collector "of the County and public taxes for the year 1796" for Hawkins County.
Territorial Papers of the US - volume: 4 page: 471
Berry, Thomas, Territory South of Ohio River, Hawkins County
        Berry, Thomas, Male

On 2 Feb 1795 he was appointed Sheriff and "Collector of the county and public taxes . . . in the Year 1795" for Hawkins County.
Territorial Papers of the US - volume: 4 page: 465
Bird, Abraham, Territory South of Ohio River, Jefferson County
        Bird, Abraham, Male
On 7 Feb 1795 he was made a Captain of the Jefferson troop in the Regiment of Cavalry for Hamilton District.
Territorial Papers of the US - volume: 4 page: 466
Black, Joseph, Territory South of Ohio River, Blount County
        Black, Joseph, Male
List, 21 Dec 1795, of members of Knoxville Convention.
Territorial Papers of the US - volume: 4 page: 415
Blackmore, George Dawson, Territory South of Ohio River, Mero District
        Blackmore, George Dawson, Male
On 16 Jan 1795 he was made Second Major of the Cavalry for Mero District.
Territorial Papers of the US - volume: 4 page: 464
Blount, William, Territory South of Ohio River, Knox County
        Blount, William, Male
List, 21 Dec 1795, of members of Knoxville Convention.
Territorial Papers of the US - volume: 4 page: 415
Blount, Willie, Territory South of Ohio River
        Blount, Willie, Male **Job:** Attorney
On 27 Oct 1795 he was "licensed to practise in the Superior Courts of Law and Courts of Equity."
Territorial Papers of the US - volume: 4 page: 470
Boatman, Henry, Tennessee, Grainger County
        Boatman, Henry, Male
"List of Taxable Property Harris Company Taken by James Moore. 1798"; Land: 208; "W[hite?] Pole": 1; "B[lack?] Pole": 0; "S[tud?] Horse": 0.
Tennessee Records of Grainger County-Tax Lists, 1798, [TN State Library and Archives] FAMILY HISTORY LIBRARY film 464105
Boatman?, George, Tennessee, Grainger County
        Boatman?, George, Male
"List of Taxable Property Harris Company Taken by James Moore. 1798"; Land: 0; "W[hite?] Pole": 1; "B[lack?] Pole": 0; "S[tud?] Horse": 0.

Tennessee Records of Grainger County-Tax Lists, 1798, [TN State Library and Archives] FAMILY HISTORY LIBRARY film 464105

Bogle, Andrew, Territory South of Ohio River, Blount County

Bogle, Andrew, Male

On 3 Aug 1795 he was made a Justice of the Peace for Blount County.

Territorial Papers of the US - volume: 4 page: 469

Bogle, Samuel, Territory South of Ohio River, Knox County

Bogle, Samuel, Male

On 3 Feb 1795 he was made a Lieutenant in the Knox Regiment of Infantry.

Territorial Papers of the US - volume: 4 page: 465

Bogle, Samuel, Territory South of Ohio River, Blount County

Bogle, Samuel, Male

On 3 Aug 1795 he was made an Ensign for Blount County.

Territorial Papers of the US - volume: 4 page: 469

Bond, Benjamin, Tennessee, Grainger County

Bond, Benjamin, Male

List of taxable property "Capt Margraves Compt 1799"; Lands: 0; "W[hite?] Poles": 1; "B[lack?] Poles": 0; "S[tud?] horses": 0; "Town Lots": 0.

Tennessee Records of Grainger County-Tax Lists, 1799, [TN State Library and Archives] FAMILY HISTORY LIBRARY film 464105

Boyd, Robert, Territory South of Ohio River, Blount County

Boyd, Robert, Male

On 3 Aug 1795 he was made an Ensign for Blount County.

Territorial Papers of the US - volume: 4 page: 469

Boyd, Robert, Territory South of Ohio River, Knox County

Boyd, Robert, Male

On 3 Feb 1795 he was made a Captain in the Knox Regiment of Infantry.

Territorial Papers of the US - volume: 4 page: 465

Branson, Semuel, Tennessee, Grainger County

Branson, Semuel, Male

"Tax List Capt Jenings District taken in by Wm Hancock. 1797"; "W[hites?]": 1; "B[lacks?]": 0; "L[and?]": 0; "S[tud?] H[orses?]": 0.

Tennessee Records of Grainger County-Tax Lists, 1797 [TN State Library and Archives] FAMILY HISTORY LIBRARY film 464105

Brazeale, Henry, Territory South of Ohio River, Knox County

Brazeale, Henry, Male

On 2 May 1795 he was appointed Deputy Sheriff for Knox County.

Territorial Papers of the US - volume: 4 page: 467

Breden, Spensur, Tennessee, Grainger County

Breden, Spensur, Male

List of taxable property "Capt Margraves Compt 1799"; Lands: 0; "W[hite?] Poles": 1; "B[lack?] Poles": 0; "S[tud?] horses": 0; "Town Lots": 0.

Tennessee Records of Grainger County-Tax Lists, 1799, [TN State Library and Archives] FAMILY HISTORY LIBRARY film 464105

Bristow, John, Tennessee, Grainger County

Bristow, John, Male

"Tax List Capt Jenings District taken in by Wm Hancock. 1797"; "W[hites?]": 1; "B[lacks?]": 0; "L[and?]": 200; "S[tud?] H[orses?]": 0.

Tennessee Records of Grainger County-Tax Lists, 1797 [TN State Library and Archives] FAMILY HISTORY LIBRARY film 464105

Brock, Alen, Jr Tennessee, Grainger County

Brock, Alen, Jr Male

"Tax List Capt Jenings District taken in by Wm Hancock. 1797"; "W[hites?]": 1; "B[lacks?]": 0; "L[and?]": 200; "S[tud?] H[orses?]": 0.

Tennessee Records of Grainger County-Tax Lists, 1797 [TN State Library and Archives] FAMILY HISTORY LIBRARY film 464105

Brock, Alen, Senr Tennessee, Grainger County

Brock, Alen, Senr Male

"Tax List Capt Jenings District taken in by Wm Hancock. 1797"; "W[hites?]": 1; "B[lacks?]": 0; "L[and?]": 137; "S[tud?] H[orses?]": 0.

Tennessee Records of Grainger County-Tax Lists, 1797 [TN State Library and Archives] FAMILY HISTORY LIBRARY film 464105

Brock, John, Tennessee, Grainger County

Brock, John, Male

"Tax List Capt Jenings District taken in by Wm Hancock. 1797"; "W[hites?]": 1; "B[lacks?]": 0; "L[and?]": 0; "S[tud?] H[orses?]": 0.

Tennessee Records of Grainger County-Tax Lists, 1797 [TN State Library and Archives]   FAMILY HISTORY LIBRARY film 464105

Brock, Moses, Tennessee, Grainger County
        Brock, Moses,   Male
List of taxable property "Capt Margraves Compt 1799"; Lands: 100; "W[hite?] Poles": 0; "B[lack?] Poles": 1; "S[tud?] horses": 0; "Town Lots": 0.
Tennessee Records of Grainger County-Tax Lists, 1799, [TN State Library and Archives]   FAMILY HISTORY LIBRARY film 464105

Brockers, William,   Tennessee,   Grainger County
        Brockers, William,   Male
List of taxable property "Capt Margraves Compt 1799"; Lands: 25; "W[hite?] Poles": 1; "B[lack?] Poles": 0; "S[tud?] horses": 0; "Town Lots": 0.
Tennessee Records of Grainger County-Tax Lists, 1799, [TN State Library and Archives]   FAMILY HISTORY LIBRARY film 464105

Broon, Thomas,   Tennessee,   Grainger County
        Broon, Thomas,   Male
List of taxable property "Capt Margraves Compt 1799"; Lands: 175; "W[hite?] Poles": 1; "B[lack?] Poles": 0; "S[tud?] horses": 0; "Town Lots": 0.
Tennessee Records of Grainger County-Tax Lists, 1799, [TN State Library and Archives]   FAMILY HISTORY LIBRARY film 464105

Brown, Edward,   Tennessee,   Grainger County
        Brown, Edward,   Male
"List of Taxable Property Harris Company Taken by James Moore. 1798"; Land: 0; "W[hite?] Pole": 1; "B[lack?] Pole": 0; "S[tud?] Horse": 0.
Tennessee Records of Grainger County-Tax Lists, 1798, [TN State Library and Archives]   FAMILY HISTORY LIBRARY film 464105

Brown, Thomas,   Tennessee,   Grainger County
        Brown, Thomas,   Male
"List of Taxable Property Harris Company Taken by James Moore. 1798"; Land: 190; "W[hite?] Pole": 1; "B[lack?] Pole": 0; "S[tud?] Horse": 0.
Page 33 is out of order and can be found on the microfilm following page 202. Page 33 has no heading, but the columns appear to be the same as those on page 32 and so will be considered as a part of that series. The entries appear to be crossed out.

Buckingham, Nathaniel,   Territory South of Ohio River, Sevier County
        Buckingham, Nathaniel,   Male
On 23 Oct 1795 he was made a Deputy Sheriff for Sevier County.
Territorial Papers of the US - volume: 4 page: 470
Buckingham, Nathaniel,   Territory South of Ohio River, Sevier County
        Buckingham, Nathaniel,   Male
On 7 Jan 1796 he was made Deputy Sheriff for Sevier County.
Territorial Papers of the US - volume: 4 page: 471
Buckingham, Thomas,   Territory South of Ohio River, Sevier County
        Buckingham, Thomas,   Male
On 2 Feb 1795 he was appointed Sheriff and "Collector of the county and public taxes . . . in the Year 1795" for Sevier County.
Territorial Papers of the US - volume: 4 page: 465
Buckingham, Thomas,   Territory South of Ohio River, Sevier County
        Buckingham, Thomas,   Male
On 2 May 1795 he was appointed Sheriff for Sevier County.
Territorial Papers of the US - volume: 4 page: 467
Buckingham, Thomas, Junior Territory South of Ohio River, Sevier County
        Buckingham, Thomas, Junior   Male
On 7 Jan 1796 he was made Sheriff for Sevier County.
Territorial Papers of the US - volume: 4 page: 470
Buckingham, Thomas, junior Territory South of Ohio River, Sevier County
        Buckingham, Thomas, junior   Male
On 27 Jan 1796 he was designated Collector "of the County and public taxes for the year 1796" for Sevier County.
Territorial Papers of the US - volume: 4 page: 471
Bull, George, Tennessee, Grainger County
        Bull, George,   Male
"Tax List Capt Jenings District taken in by Wm Hancock. 1797"; "W[hites?]": 1; "B[lacks?]": 0; "L[and?]": 0; "S[tud?] H[orses?]": 0.
Tennessee Records of Grainger County-Tax Lists, 1797 [TN State Library and Archives]   FAMILY HISTORY LIBRARY film 464105

Bunch, Charles, Tennessee, Grainger County
Bunch, Charles, Male
"List of Taxable Property Harris Company Taken by James Moore. 1798"; Land: ?; "W[hite?] Pole": ?; "B[lack?] Pole": 0; "S[tud?] Horse": 0.
Tennessee Records of Grainger County-Tax Lists, 1798, [TN State Library and Archives] FAMILY HISTORY LIBRARY film 464105
Bunch, David, Tennessee, Grainger County
Bunch, David, Male
"Tax List Capt Jenings District taken in by Wm Hancock. 1797"; "W[hites?]": 1?; "B[lacks?]": 0; "L[and?]": 1**; "S[tud?] H[orses?]": 0.
Tennessee Records of Grainger County-Tax Lists, 1797 [TN State Library and Archives] FAMILY HISTORY LIBRARY film 464105
Bunch, John, Tennessee, Grainger County
Bunch, John, Male
"Tax List Capt Jenings District taken in by Wm Hancock. 1797"; "W[hites?]": 1; "B[lacks?]": 0; "L[and?]": 0; "S[tud?] H[orses?]": 0.
Tennessee Records of Grainger County-Tax Lists, 1797 [TN State Library and Archives] FAMILY HISTORY LIBRARY film 464105
Bunch, John, Tennessee, Grainger County
Bunch, John, Male
"List of Taxable Property Harris Company Taken by James Moore. 1798"; Land: 320; "W[hite?] Pole": 1; "B[lack?] Pole": 0; "S[tud?] Horse": 0.
Tennessee Records of Grainger County-Tax Lists, 1798, [TN State Library and Archives] FAMILY HISTORY LIBRARY film 464105
Burd, John, Tennessee, Grainger County
Burd, John, Male
"List of Taxable Property Harris Company Taken by James Moore. 1798"; Land: 100; "W[hite?] Pole": 1; "B[lack?] Pole": 1; "S[tud?] Horse": 0.
Tennessee Records of Grainger County-Tax Lists, 1798, [TN State Library and Archives] FAMILY HISTORY LIBRARY film 464105
Burtain, William, Tennessee, Grainger County
Burtain, William, Male
List of taxable property "Capt Margraves Compt 1799"; Lands: 250; "W[hite?] Poles": 1; "B[lack?] Poles": 0; "S[tud?] horses": 0; "Town Lots": 0.
Tennessee Records of Grainger County-Tax Lists, 1799, [TN State Library and Archives] FAMILY HISTORY LIBRARY film 464105

Burton, William, Tennessee, Grainger County
Burton, William, Male
"List of Taxable Property Harris Company Taken by James Moore. 1798"; Land: 0; "W[hite?] Pole": 1; "B[lack?] Pole": 0; "S[tud?] Horse": 0.
Page 33 is out of order and can be found on the microfilm following page 202. Page 33 has no heading, but the columns appear to be the same as those on page 32 and so will be considered as a part of that series. The entries appear to be crossed out.
Tennessee Records of Grainger County-Tax Lists, 1798, [TN State Library and Archives] FAMILY HISTORY LIBRARY film 464105
Byrnes, James, Territory South of Ohio River, Davidson County
Byrnes, James, Male
On 11 Jul 1795 he was made a Justice of the Peace for Davidson County.
Territorial Papers of the US - volume: 4 page: 468
Cabbage, Adam, Tennessee, Grainger County
Cabbage, Adam, Male
"Tax List Capt Jenings District taken in by Wm Hancock. 1797"; "W[hites?]": 1; "B[lacks?]": 0; "L[and?]": 100; "S[tud?] H[orses?]": 0.
Tennessee Records of Grainger County-Tax Lists, 1797 [TN State Library and Archives] FAMILY HISTORY LIBRARY film 464105
Cabbage, John, Tennessee, Grainger County
Cabbage, John, Male
"Tax List Capt Jenings District taken in by Wm Hancock. 1797"; "W[hites?]": 1; "B[lacks?]": 0; "L[and?]": 100; "S[tud?] H[orses?]": 0.
Tennessee Records of Grainger County-Tax Lists, 1797 [TN State Library and Archives] FAMILY HISTORY LIBRARY film 464105
Cage, Reuben, Territory South of Ohio River, Sumner County
Cage, Reuben, Male
On 27 Jan 1796 he was designated Collector "of the County and public taxes for the year 1796" for Sumner County.
Territorial Papers of the US - volume: 4 page: 471
Cage, Reuben, Territory South of Ohio River, Sumner County
Cage, Reuben, Male

On 6 Jul 1795 he was made Sheriff for Sumner County.
Territorial Papers of the US - volume: 4 page: 468
Cage, William, Territory South of Ohio River, Sumner County
Cage, William, Male
On 2 Feb 1795 he was appointed Sheriff and "Collector of the county and public taxes . . . in the Year 1795" for Sumner County.
Territorial Papers of the US - volume: 4 page: 465
Cage, Wilson, Territory South of Ohio River, Mero District
Cage, Wilson, Male
On 17 Jan 1795 he was made a Lieutenant of the Cavalry for Mero District.
Territorial Papers of the US - volume: 4 page: 464
Carmichael, Dunkin, Tennessee, Grainger County
Carmichael, Dunkin, Male
"List of Taxable Property Harris Company Taken by James Moore. 1798"; Land: 400; "W[hite?] Pole": 1; "B[lack?] Pole": 0; "S[tud?] Horse": 0.
Tennessee Records of Grainger County-Tax Lists, 1798, [TN State Library and Archives] FAMILY HISTORY LIBRARY film 464105
Cassey, James, Tennessee, Grainger County
Cassey, James, Male
"Tax List Capt Jenings District taken in by Wm Hancock. 1797"; "W[hites?]": 1; "B[lacks?]": 0; "L[and?]": 0; "S[tud?] H[orses?]": 0.
Tennessee Records of Grainger County-Tax Lists, 1797 [TN State Library and Archives] FAMILY HISTORY LIBRARY film 464105
Cassey, John, Tennessee, Grainger County
Cassey, John, Male
"Tax List Capt Jenings District taken in by Wm Hancock. 1797"; "W[hites?]": 1; "B[lacks?]": 0; "L[and?]": 200; "S[tud?] H[orses?]": 0.
Tennessee Records of Grainger County-Tax Lists, 1797 [TN State Library and Archives] FAMILY HISTORY LIBRARY film 464105
Chambelin, Mary, Tennessee, Grainger County
Chambelin, Mary, Female
"List of Taxable Property Harris Company Taken by James Moore. 1798"; Land: 240; "W[hite?] Pole": 0; "B[lack?] Pole": 0; "S[tud?] Horse": 0.

Tennessee Records of Grainger County-Tax Lists, 1798, [TN State Library and Archives] FAMILY HISTORY LIBRARY film 464105
Chamberlin, Elizabeth, Tennessee, Grainger County
Chamberlin, Elizabeth, Female
"List of Taxable Property Harris Company Taken by James Moore. 1798"; Land: 289; "W[hite?] Pole": 0; "B[lack?] Pole": 0; "S[tud?] Horse": 0.
Tennessee Records of Grainger County-Tax Lists, 1798, [TN State Library and Archives] FAMILY HISTORY LIBRARY film 464105
Chamberlin, Jennet, Tennessee, Grainger County
Chamberlin, Jennet, Female
"List of Taxable Property Harris Company Taken by James Moore. 1798"; Land: 267; "W[hite?] Pole": 0; "B[lack?] Pole": 0; "S[tud?] Horse": 0.
Tennessee Records of Grainger County-Tax Lists, 1798, [TN State Library and Archives] FAMILY HISTORY LIBRARY film 464105
Chamberlin, Jermia, Tennessee, Grainger County
Chamberlin, Jermia, Male
"List of Taxable Property Harris Company Taken by James Moore. 1798"; Land: 700; "W[hite?] Pole": 1; "B[lack?] Pole": 0; "S[tud?] Horse": 0.
Tennessee Records of Grainger County-Tax Lists, 1798, [TN State Library and Archives] FAMILY HISTORY LIBRARY film 464105
Chamberlin, John, Tennessee, Grainger County
Chamberlin, John, Male
"List of Taxable Property Harris Company Taken by James Moore. 1798"; Land: 253; "W[hite?] Pole": 0; "B[lack?] Pole": 0; "S[tud?] Horse": 0.
Tennessee Records of Grainger County-Tax Lists, 1798, [TN State Library and Archives] FAMILY HISTORY LIBRARY film 464105
Chamberlin, Margaret, Tennessee, Grainger County
Chamberlin, Margaret, Female
"List of Taxable Property Harris Company Taken by James Moore. 1798"; Land: 250; "W[hite?] Pole": 0; "B[lack?] Pole": 0; "S[tud?] Horse": 0.
Tennessee Records of Grainger County-Tax Lists, 1798, [TN State Library and Archives] FAMILY HISTORY LIBRARY film 464105
Chaston, William, Tennessee, Grainger County

Chaston, William,   Male
List of taxable property "Capt Margraves Compt 1799"; Lands: 150; "W[hite?] Poles": 1; "B[lack?] Poles": 0; "S[tud?] horses": 0; "Town Lots": 0.
Tennessee Records of Grainger County-Tax Lists, 1799, [TN State Library and Archives]   FAMILY HISTORY LIBRARY film 464105
Cheak, Dosson,   Tennessee,   Grainger County
      Cheak, Dosson,   Male
"Tax List Capt Jenings District taken in by Wm Hancock. 1797"; "W[hites?]": 1; "B[lacks?]": 0; "L[and?]": 100; "S[tud?] H[orses?]": 0.
Tennessee Records of Grainger County-Tax Lists, 1797 [TN State Library and Archives]   FAMILY HISTORY LIBRARY film 464105
Childers, William,   Territory South of Ohio River, Sullivan County
      Childers, William,   Male
On 31 Jan 1795 he was appointed Second Major of the Sullivan Regiment of Infantry.
Territorial Papers of the US - volume: 4 page: 465
Chisholm, James,   Territory South of Ohio River, Hawkins County
      Chisholm, James,   Male
On 1 Aug 1795 he was made a Lieutenant in the militia for Hawkins County.
Territorial Papers of the US - volume: 4 page: 469
Christian, Jesse,   Tennessee,   Grainger County
      Christian, Jesse,   Male
"List of Taxable Property Harris Company Taken by James Moore. 1798"; Land: 50; "W[hite?] Pole": 0; "B[lack?] Pole": 0; "S[tud?] Horse": 0.
Tennessee Records of Grainger County-Tax Lists, 1798, [TN State Library and Archives]   FAMILY HISTORY LIBRARY film 464105
Circle? "Sircle", George,   Tennessee, Grainger County
      Circle? "Sircle", George,   Male
"Tax List Capt Jenings District taken in by Wm Hancock. 1797"; "W[hites?]": 1; "B[lacks?]": 0; "L[and?]": 320; "S[tud?] H[orses?]": 0.
Tennessee Records of Grainger County-Tax Lists, 1797 [TN State Library and Archives]   FAMILY HISTORY LIBRARY film 464105
Clack, John,   Territory South of Ohio River, Sevier County
      Clack, John,   Male
On 15 Jul 1795 he was made a Justice of the Peace for Sevier County.
Territorial Papers of the US - volume: 4 page: 468
Claiborne, William Charles Cole,   Territory South of Ohio River, Sullivan County
      Claiborne, William Charles Cole,   Male
On 14 Nov 1795 "William Charles Cole Claiborne of the County of Sullivan [was] appointed Brigade Major of the Brigade commanded by Brigadier General John Sevier."
Territorial Papers of the US - volume: 4 page: 470
Clark, Edward,   Tennessee,   Grainger County
      Clark, Edward, Male
"Tax List Capt Jenings District taken in by Wm Hancock. 1797"; "W[hites?]": 1; "B[lacks?]": 0; "L[and?]": 320; "S[tud?] H[orses?]": 0.
Tennessee Records of Grainger County-Tax Lists, 1797 [TN State Library and Archives]   FAMILY HISTORY LIBRARY film 464105
Clark, Samuel,   Tennessee,   Grainger County
      Clark, Samuel, Male
"Tax List Capt Jenings District taken in by Wm Hancock. 1797"; "W[hites?]": 1; "B[lacks?]": 0; "L[and?]": 90; "S[tud?] H[orses?]": 0.
Tennessee Records of Grainger County-Tax Lists, 1797 [TN State Library and Archives]   FAMILY HISTORY LIBRARY film 464105
Clay, Wm,   Tennessee, Grainger County
      Clay, Wm,   Male
"List of Taxable Property Harris Company Taken by James Moore. 1798"; Land: 108; "W[hite?] Pole": 1; "B[lack?] Pole": 0; "S[tud?] Horse": 0.
Tennessee Records of Grainger County-Tax Lists, 1798, [TN State Library and Archives]   FAMILY HISTORY LIBRARY film 464105
Clonch, Barnet,   Tennessee,   Grainger County
      Clonch, Barnet,   Male
"Tax List Capt Jenings District taken in by Wm Hancock. 1797"; "W[hites?]": 1; "B[lacks?]": 0; "L[and?]": ?; "S[tud?] H[orses?]": 0.
Tennessee Records of Grainger County-Tax Lists, 1797 [TN State Library and Archives]   FAMILY HISTORY LIBRARY film 464105
Clonch, John,   Tennessee, Grainger County
      Clonch, John,   Male

"Tax List Capt Jenings District taken in by Wm Hancock. 1797"; "W[hites?]": 1; "B[lacks?]": 0; "L[and?]": 0; "S[tud?] H[orses?]": 0.
Tennessee Records of Grainger County-Tax Lists, 1797 [TN State Library and Archives] FAMILY HISTORY LIBRARY film 464105
Coats, Benjamin,   Tennessee,   Grainger County
          Coats, Benjamin,   Male
List of taxable property "Capt Margraves Compt 1799"; Lands: 0; "W[hite?] Poles": 1; "B[lack?] Poles": 0; "S[tud?] horses": 0; "Town Lots": 0.
Tennessee Records of Grainger County-Tax Lists, 1799, [TN State Library and Archives] FAMILY HISTORY LIBRARY film 464105
Cochran, John,   Territory South of Ohio River, Blount County
          Cochran, John, Male
On 3 Aug 1795 he was made an Ensign for Blount County.
Territorial Papers of the US - volume: 4 page: 469
Cocke, John, Esquire Territory South of Ohio River
          Cocke, John, Esquire   Male   **Job:** Attorney
On 24 Oct 1795 he was "licensed to practise as an Attorney at Law in the Superior Courts of Law and Courts of Equity."
Territorial Papers of the US - volume: 4 page: 470
Coffee, Meridy,   Tennessee,   Grainger County
          Coffee, Meridy,   Male
          Female?
"List of Taxable Property Harris Company Taken by James Moore. 1798"; Land: 0; "W[hite?] Pole": 1; "B[lack?] Pole": 0; "S[tud?] Horse": 0.
Tennessee Records of Grainger County-Tax Lists, 1798, [TN State Library and Archives] FAMILY HISTORY LIBRARY film 464105
Collison, James, Jr Tennessee,   Grainger County
          Collison, James, Jr   Male
"List of Taxable Property Harris Company Taken by James Moore. 1798"; Land: 300; "W[hite?] Pole": 1; "B[lack?] Pole": 0; "S[tud?] Horse": 0.
Tennessee Records of Grainger County-Tax Lists, 1798, [TN State Library and Archives] FAMILY HISTORY LIBRARY film 464105
Conner, John, Tennessee, Grainger County
          Conner, John, Male

"List of Taxable Property Harris Company Taken by James Moore. 1798"; Land: 0; "W[hite?] Pole": 1; "B[lack?] Pole": 0; "S[tud?] Horse": 0.
Page 33 is out of order and can be found on the microfilm following page 202. Page 33 has no heading, but the columns appear to be the same as those on page 32 and so will be considered as a part of that series. The entries appear to be crossed out.
Tennessee Records of Grainger County-Tax Lists, 1798, [TN State Library and Archives] FAMILY HISTORY LIBRARY film 464105
Conway, George,   Territory South of Ohio River, Greene County
          Conway, George,   Male
On 2 May 1795 he was made Sheriff "and Collector of Taxes" for Greene County in the place of William Conway who resigned.
Territorial Papers of the US - volume: 4 page: 467
Conway, George,   Territory South of Ohio River, Greene County
          Conway, George,   Male
On 27 Jan 1796 he was designated Collector "of the County and public taxes for the year 1796" for Greene County.
Territorial Papers of the US - volume: 4 page: 471
Conway, William,   Territory South of Ohio River, Greene County
          Conway, William,   Male
On 2 Feb 1795 he was appointed Sheriff and "Collector of the county and public taxes . . . in the Year 1795" for Greene County.
Territorial Papers of the US - volume: 4 page: 465
Conway, William,   Territory South of Ohio River, Greene County
          Conway, William,   Male
He was replaced by George Conway, 2 May 1795, because he resigned from serving as Sheriff "and Collector of Taxes" for Greene County.
Territorial Papers of the US - volume: 4 page: 467
Conway, William,   Territory South of Ohio River   Washington District
          Conway, William,   Male
On 27 Nov 1795 he was "appointed Second Lieutenant of Cavalry in the Regiment of Washington District."
Territorial Papers of the US - volume: 4 page: 470
Cotner, Pether,   Tennessee,   Grainger County
          Cotner, Pether, Male

"List of Taxable Property Harris Company Taken by James Moore. 1798"; Land: 150; "W[hite?] Pole": 0; "B[lack?] Pole": 0; "S[tud?] Horse": 0.
Tennessee Records of Grainger County-Tax Lists, 1798, [TN State Library and Archives] FAMILY HISTORY LIBRARY film 464105

Couley, John, Tennessee, Grainger County
     Couley, John,   Male
"List of Taxable Property Harris Company Taken by James Moore. 1798"; Land: ?; "W[hite?] Pole": ?; "B[lack?] Pole": 0; "S[tud?] Horse": 0.
Tennessee Records of Grainger County-Tax Lists, 1798, [TN State Library and Archives] FAMILY HISTORY LIBRARY film 464105

Counts, John, Tennessee, Grainger County
     Counts, John,   Male
"List of Taxable Property Harris Company Taken by James Moore. 1798"; Land: 200; "W[hite?] Pole": 1; "B[lack?] Pole": 0; "S[tud?] Horse": 0.
Tennessee Records of Grainger County-Tax Lists, 1798, [TN State Library and Archives] FAMILY HISTORY LIBRARY film 464105

Craig, Daniel, Territory South of Ohio River, Blount County
     Craig, Daniel,   Male
List, 21 Dec 1795, of members of Knoxville Convention.
Territorial Papers of the US - volume: 4 page: 415

Craig, David, Territory South of Ohio River, Blount County
     Craig, David,   Male
On 3 Aug 1795 he was made a Justice of the Peace for Blount County.
Territorial Papers of the US - volume: 4 page: 469

Crawford, John, Territory South of Ohio River, Knox County
     Crawford, John,   Male
List, 21 Dec 1795, of members of Knoxville Convention.
Territorial Papers of the US - volume: 4 page: 415

Culveghor, William, Tennessee, Grainger County
     Culveghor, William,   Male
List of taxable property "Capt Margraves Compt 1799"; Lands: 250; "W[hite?] Poles": 0; "B[lack?] Poles": 0; "S[tud?] horses": 0; "Town Lots": 0.
Tennessee Records of Grainger County-Tax Lists, 1799, [TN State Library and Archives] FAMILY HISTORY LIBRARY film 464105

Cunningham, James, Territory South of Ohio River, Blount County
     Cunningham, James,   Male
On 3 Aug 1795 he was made a Captain in the Cavalry for Blount County.
Territorial Papers of the US - volume: 4 page: 469

Cunningham, James, Territory South of Ohio River, Hamilton District
     Cunningham, James,   Male
On 27 Jan 1795 he was made a First Lieutenant in the Regiment of Cavalry for Hamilton District.
Territorial Papers of the US - volume: 4 page: 464

Curnham, Ivy, Tennessee, Grainger County
     Curnham, Ivy,   Female
List of taxable property "Capt Margraves Compt 1799"; Lands: 0; "W[hite?] Poles": 1; "B[lack?] Poles": 0; "S[tud?] horses": 0; "Town Lots": 0.
Tennessee Records of Grainger County-Tax Lists, 1799, [TN State Library and Archives] FAMILY HISTORY LIBRARY film 464105

Dale, Abel, Tennessee, Grainger County
     Dale, Abel,   Male
List of taxable property "Capt Margraves Compt 1799"; Lands: 600; "W[hite?] Poles": 0; "B[lack?] Poles": 0; "S[tud?] horses": 0; "Town Lots": 0.
Tennessee Records of Grainger County-Tax Lists, 1799, [TN State Library and Archives] FAMILY HISTORY LIBRARY film 464105

Dale, Able, Tennessee, Grainger County
     Dale, Able,   Male
"List of Taxable Property Harris Company Taken by James Moore. 1798"; Land: 500; "W[hite?] Pole": 1; "B[lack?] Pole": 0; "S[tud?] Horse": 0.
Page 33 is out of order and can be found on the microfilm following page 202. Page 33 has no heading, but the columns appear to be the same as those on page 32 and so will be considered as a part of that series. The entries appear to be crossed out.
Tennessee Records of Grainger County-Tax Lists, 1798, [TN State Library and Archives] FAMILY HISTORY LIBRARY film 464105

Davidson, John, Tennessee, Grainger County
     Davidson, John,   Male
List of taxable property "Capt Margraves Compt 1799"; Lands: 200; "W[hite?] Poles": 0; "B[lack?] Poles": 0; "S[tud?] horses": 0; "Town Lots": 0.

Tennessee Records of Grainger County-Tax Lists, 1799, [TN State Library and Archives] FAMILY HISTORY LIBRARY film 464105

Davis, George, Tennessee, Grainger County
  Davis, George, Male
"List of Taxable Property Harris Company Taken by James Moore. 1798"; Land: 0; "W[hite?] Pole": 1; "B[lack?] Pole": 0; "S[tud?] Horse": 0.
Tennessee Records of Grainger County-Tax Lists, 1798, [TN State Library and Archives] FAMILY HISTORY LIBRARY film 464105

Davison, Edward, Tennessee, Grainger County
  Davison, Edward, Male
List of taxable property "Capt Margraves Compt 1799"; Lands: 200; "W[hite?] Poles": 0; "B[lack?] Poles": 0; "S[tud?] horses": 0; "Town Lots": 0.
Tennessee Records of Grainger County-Tax Lists, 1799, [TN State Library and Archives] FAMILY HISTORY LIBRARY film 464105

Deaderick, John, Territory South of Ohio River, Davidson County
  Deaderick, John, Male
On 11 Jul 1795 he was made a Justice of the Peace for Davidson County.
Territorial Papers of the US - volume: 4 page: 468

Dennis, John, Tennessee, Grainger County
  Dennis, John, Male
List of taxable property "Capt Margraves Compt 1799"; Lands: 0; "W[hite?] Poles": 1; "B[lack?] Poles": 0; "S[tud?] horses": 0; "Town Lots": 0.
Tennessee Records of Grainger County-Tax Lists, 1799, [TN State Library and Archives] FAMILY HISTORY LIBRARY film 464105

Dennis, Joseph, Tennessee, Grainger County
  Dennis, Joseph, Male
List of taxable property "Capt Margraves Compt 1799"; Lands: 80; "W[hite?] Poles": 1; "B[lack?] Poles": 0; "S[tud?] horses": 0; "Town Lots": 0.
Tennessee Records of Grainger County-Tax Lists, 1799, [TN State Library and Archives] FAMILY HISTORY LIBRARY film 464105

Dennis, Joseph, Tennessee, Grainger County
  Dennis, Joseph, Male
"List of Taxable Property Harris Company Taken by James Moore. 1798"; Land: 82; "W[hite?] Pole": 1; "B[lack?] Pole": 0; "S[tud?] Horse": 0.

Page 33 is out of order and can be found on the microfilm following page 202. Page 33 has no heading, but the columns appear to be the same as those on page 32 and so will be considered as a part of that series. The entries appear to be crossed out.
Tennessee Records of Grainger County-Tax Lists, 1798, [TN State Library and Archives] FAMILY HISTORY LIBRARY film 464105

Dennis, Robert, Tennessee, Grainger County
  Dennis, Robert, Male
"List of Taxable Property Harris Company Taken by James Moore. 1798"; Land: 240; "W[hite?] Pole": 0; "B[lack?] Pole": 0; "S[tud?] Horse": 0.
Tennessee Records of Grainger County-Tax Lists, 1798, [TN State Library and Archives] FAMILY HISTORY LIBRARY film 464105

Dennis, Thomas, Tennessee, Grainger County
  Dennis, Thomas, Male
List of taxable property "Capt Margraves Compt 1799"; Lands: 200; "W[hite?] Poles": 1; "B[lack?] Poles": 0; "S[tud?] horses": 0; "Town Lots": 0.
Tennessee Records of Grainger County-Tax Lists, 1799, [TN State Library and Archives] FAMILY HISTORY LIBRARY film 464105

Devaul, Jacob, Tennessee, Grainger County
  Devaul, Jacob, Male
List of taxable property "Capt Margraves Compt 1799"; Lands: 200; "W[hite?] Poles": 0; "B[lack?] Poles": 0; "S[tud?] horses": 0; "Town Lots": 0.
Tennessee Records of Grainger County-Tax Lists, 1799, [TN State Library and Archives] FAMILY HISTORY LIBRARY film 464105

Dilliard, Benjamin, Territory South of Ohio River, Washington County
  Dilliard, Benjamin, Male
On 11 Jul 1795 he was made a Justice of the Peace for Washington County.
Territorial Papers of the US - volume: 4 page: 468

Doack, Samuel, Territory South of Ohio River, Knox County
  Doack, Samuel, Male
On 1 Aug 1795 he was made a Justice of the Peace for Knox County.
Territorial Papers of the US - volume: 4 page: 468

Dodson, John, Tennessee, Grainger County
  Dodson, John, Male

"Tax List Capt Jenings District taken in by Wm Hancock. 1797"; "W[hites?]": 1; "B[lacks?]": 0; "L[and?]": 0; "S[tud?] H[orses?]": 0.
Tennessee Records of Grainger County-Tax Lists, 1797 [TN State Library and Archives]   FAMILY HISTORY LIBRARY film 464105
Dodson, Samuel,   Tennessee,   Grainger County
          Dodson, Samuel,   Male
"Tax List Capt Jenings District taken in by Wm Hancock. 1797"; "W[hites?]": 1; "B[lacks?]": 0; "L[and?]": 0; "S[tud?] H[orses?]": 0.
Tennessee Records of Grainger County-Tax Lists, 1797 [TN State Library and Archives]   FAMILY HISTORY LIBRARY film 464105
Doherty, , Col: Territory South of Ohio River, Jefferson County
          Doherty, , Col: Male
List, 21 Dec 1795, of members of Knoxville Convention.
Territorial Papers of the US - volume: 4 page: 415
Donald, Thomas,   Territory South of Ohio River, Sumner County
          Donald, Thomas,   Male
On 2 Mar 1795 he was made a Justice of the Peace for Sumner County.
Territorial Papers of the US - volume: 4 page: 467
Donelson, Samuel, Esquire   Territory South of Ohio River
          Donelson, Samuel, Esquire   Male
          Job: Attorney
On 5 Dec 1795 he was "licensed to practise as an Attorney in the Superior Courts of Law and Courts of Equity."
Territorial Papers of the US - volume: 4 page: 470
Dotson, William,   Tennessee,   Grainger County
          Dotson, William,   Male
List of taxable property "Capt Margraves Compt 1799"; Lands: 0; "W[hite?] Poles": 1; "B[lack?] Poles": 0; "S[tud?] horses": 0; "Town Lots": 0.
Tennessee Records of Grainger County-Tax Lists, 1799, [TN State Library and Archives]   FAMILY HISTORY LIBRARY film 464105
Douglass, Edward,   Territory South of Ohio River, Sumner County
          Douglass, Edward,   Male
On 16 Jan 1795 he was made Lieutenant Colonel of the Infantry for Sumner County.
Territorial Papers of the US - volume: 4 page: 464

Douglass, Reuben,   Territory South of Ohio River, Mero District
          Douglass, Reuben,   Male
On 17 Jan 1795 he was made a Captain of the Cavalry for Mero District.
Territorial Papers of the US - volume: 4 page: 464
Dunkin, Wm, Tennessee, Grainger County
          Dunkin, Wm,   Male
"List of Taxable Property Harris Company Taken by James Moore. 1798"; Land: 0; "W[hite?] Pole": 1; "B[lack?] Pole": 0; "S[tud?] Horse": 0.
Tennessee Records of Grainger County-Tax Lists, 1798, [TN State Library and Archives]   FAMILY HISTORY LIBRARY film 464105
Dunn, Thomas,   Tennessee,   Grainger County
          Dunn, Thomas, Male
"Tax List Capt Jenings District taken in by Wm Hancock. 1797"; "W[hites?]": 1; "B[lacks?]": 0; "L[and?]": 200; "S[tud?] H[orses?]": 0.
Tennessee Records of Grainger County-Tax Lists, 1797 [TN State Library and Archives]   FAMILY HISTORY LIBRARY film 464105
Eakers, Jepley,   Tennessee,   Grainger County
          Eakers, Jepley, Male
"List of Taxable Property Harris Company Taken by James Moore. 1798"; Land: 0; "W[hite?] Pole": 1; "B[lack?] Pole": 0; "S[tud?] Horse": 0.
Tennessee Records of Grainger County-Tax Lists, 1798, [TN State Library and Archives]   FAMILY HISTORY LIBRARY film 464105
Ealet, Benjamin,   Tennessee,   Grainger County
          Ealet, Benjamin,   Male
"List of Taxable Property Harris Company Taken by James Moore. 1798"; Land: 0; "W[hite?] Pole": 1; "B[lack?] Pole": 0; "S[tud?] Horse": 0.
Tennessee Records of Grainger County-Tax Lists, 1798, [TN State Library and Archives]   FAMILY HISTORY LIBRARY film 464105
Eallot, Jacob, Tennessee, Grainger County
          Eallot, Jacob,   Male
"List of Taxable Property Harris Company Taken by James Moore. 1798"; Land: 0; "W[hite?] Pole": 1; "B[lack?] Pole": 0; "S[tud?] Horse": 0.
Tennessee Records of Grainger County-Tax Lists, 1798, [TN State Library and Archives]   FAMILY HISTORY LIBRARY film 464105
Eaton, Joseph, Tennessee, Grainger County

Eaton, Joseph, Male
"List of Taxable Property Harris Company Taken by James Moore. 1798"; Land: 172; "W[hite?] Pole": 0; "B[lack?] Pole": 0; "S[tud?] Horse": 0.
Tennessee Records of Grainger County-Tax Lists, 1798, [TN State Library and Archives] FAMILY HISTORY LIBRARY film 464105

Elliot, Abraham,   Tennessee,   Grainger County
Elliot, Abraham,   Male
List of taxable property "Capt Margraves Compt 1799"; Lands: 733; "W[hite?] Poles": 1; "B[lack?] Poles": 0; "S[tud?] horses": 0; "Town Lots": 0.
Tennessee Records of Grainger County-Tax Lists, 1799, [TN State Library and Archives] FAMILY HISTORY LIBRARY film 464105

Elliot, Elezbeth,   Tennessee,   Grainger County
Elliot, Elezbeth,   Female
List of taxable property "Capt Margraves Compt 1799"; Lands: 67; "W[hite?] Poles": 0; "B[lack?] Poles": 0; "S[tud?] horses": 0; "Town Lots": 0.
Tennessee Records of Grainger County-Tax Lists, 1799, [TN State Library and Archives] FAMILY HISTORY LIBRARY film 464105

Elliot, Jacob,   Tennessee, Grainger County
Elliot, Jacob,   Male
List of taxable property "Capt Margraves Compt 1799"; Lands: 333; "W[hite?] Poles": 0; "B[lack?] Poles": 0; "S[tud?] horses": 0; "Town Lots": 0.
Tennessee Records of Grainger County-Tax Lists, 1799, [TN State Library and Archives] FAMILY HISTORY LIBRARY film 464105

Elliot, Mary,   Tennessee, Grainger County
Elliot, Mary,   Female
List of taxable property "Capt Margraves Compt 1799"; Lands: 60; "W[hite?] Poles": 0; "B[lack?] Poles": 0; "S[tud?] horses": 0; "Town Lots": 0.
Tennessee Records of Grainger County-Tax Lists, 1799, [TN State Library and Archives] FAMILY HISTORY LIBRARY film 464105

Evans, Joseph,   Territory South of Ohio River, Hamilton District
Evans, Joseph, Male
On 7 Feb 1795 he was made a Captain in the Regiment of Cavalry for Hamilton District.
Territorial Papers of the US - volume: 4 page: 466

Evans, Nathaniel,   Territory South of Ohio River, Hamilton District
Evans, Nathaniel,   Male

On 7 Feb 1795 he was made First Major in the Regiment of Cavalry for Hamilton District.
Territorial Papers of the US - volume: 4 page: 466

Ewin, George, Territory South of Ohio River, Blount County
Ewin, George, Male
On 3 Aug 1795 he was made a Captain for Blount County.
Territorial Papers of the US - volume: 4 page: 469

Ewin, George, Territory South of Ohio River, Blount County
Ewin, George, Male
On 3 Aug 1795 he was made a Justice of the Peace for Blount County.
Territorial Papers of the US - volume: 4 page: 469

Fields, Joseph, Tennessee, Grainger County
Fields, Joseph, Male
List of taxable property "Capt Margraves Compt 1799"; Lands: 500; "W[hite?] Poles": 1; "B[lack?] Poles": 0; "S[tud?] horses": 0; "Town Lots": 0.
Tennessee Records of Grainger County-Tax Lists, 1799, [TN State Library and Archives] FAMILY HISTORY LIBRARY film 464105

Fields, Joseph, Tennessee, Grainger County
Fields, Joseph, Male
"List of Taxable Property Harris Company Taken by James Moore. 1798"; Land: 90; "W[hite?] Pole": 1; "B[lack?] Pole": 0; "S[tud?] Horse": 0.
Page 33 is out of order and can be found on the microfilm following page 202. Page 33 has no heading, but the columns appear to be the same as those on page 32 and so will be considered as a part of that series. The entries appear to be crossed out.
Tennessee Records of Grainger County-Tax Lists, 1798, [TN State Library and Archives] FAMILY HISTORY LIBRARY film 464105

Fields, Robert,   Tennessee,   Grainger County
Fields, Robert, Male
"List of Taxable Property Harris Company Taken by James Moore. 1798"; Land: 210; "W[hite?] Pole": 1; "B[lack?] Pole": 0; "S[tud?] Horse": 0.
Page 33 is out of order and can be found on the microfilm following page 202. Page 33 has no heading, but the columns appear to be the same as those on page 32 and so will be considered as a part of that series. The entries appear to be crossed out.

Tennessee Records of Grainger County-Tax Lists, 1798, [TN State Library and Archives]   FAMILY HISTORY LIBRARY film 464105

Frazer, James,   Territory South of Ohio River, Sumner County

Frazer, James,   Male

On 17 Jan 1795 he was made First Major in the Regiment of Infantry for Sumner County.

Territorial Papers of the US - volume: 4 page: 464

Gibbs, Nicholas,   Territory South of Ohio River, Knox County

Gibbs, Nicholas,   Male

On 13 Jul 1795 he was made a Justice of the Peace for Knox County.

Territorial Papers of the US - volume: 4 page: 468

Gibson, Archillis,   Tennessee,   Grainger County

Gibson, Archillis,   Male

"List of Taxable Property Harris Company Taken by James Moore. 1798"; Land: 100; "W[hite?] Pole": 1; "B[lack?] Pole": 0; "S[tud?] Horse": 0.

Tennessee Records of Grainger County-Tax Lists, 1798, [TN State Library and Archives]   FAMILY HISTORY LIBRARY film 464105

Gillaspie, George,   Territory South of Ohio River, Washington County

Gillaspie, George,   Male

On 2 Feb 1795 he was appointed Sheriff and "Collector of the county and public taxes . . . in the Year 1795" for Washington County.

Territorial Papers of the US - volume: 4 page: 465

Gillaspie, George,   Territory South of Ohio River, Washington County

Gillaspie, George,   Male

On 27 Jan 1796 he was designated Collector "of the County and public taxes for the year 1796" for Washington County.

Territorial Papers of the US - volume: 4 page: 471

Gillaspie, George,   Territory South of Ohio River, Washington County

Gillaspie, George,   Male

On 2 May 1795 he was appointed Sheriff for Washington County.

Territorial Papers of the US - volume: 4 page: 467

Gillinton, Nicholas,   Tennessee,   Grainger County

Gillinton, Nicholas,   Male

"Tax List Capt Jenings District taken in by Wm Hancock. 1797"; "W[hites?]": 1; "B[lacks?]": 0; "L[and?]": 0; "S[tud?] H[orses?]": 0.

Tennessee Records of Grainger County-Tax Lists, 1797 [TN State Library and Archives]   FAMILY HISTORY LIBRARY film 464105

Gilmore, John,   Tennessee,   Grainger County

Gilmore, John,   Male

"List of Taxable Property Harris Company Taken by James Moore. 1798"; Land: 350; "W[hite?] Pole": 0; "B[lack?] Pole": 0; "S[tud?] Horse": 0.

Tennessee Records of Grainger County-Tax Lists, 1798, [TN State Library and Archives]   FAMILY HISTORY LIBRARY film 464105

Gilmore, John, Jr.   Tennessee,   Grainger County

Gilmore, John, Jr.   Male

"List of Taxable Property Harris Company Taken by James Moore. 1798"; Land: 200; "W[hite?] Pole": 1; "B[lack?] Pole": 0; "S[tud?] Horse": 0.

Tennessee Records of Grainger County-Tax Lists, 1798, [TN State Library and Archives]   FAMILY HISTORY LIBRARY film 464105

Ginings, Rial,   Tennessee, Grainger County

Ginings, Rial,   Male

"Tax List Capt Jenings District taken in by Wm Hancock. 1797"; "W[hites?]": 1; "B[lacks?]": 0; "L[and?]": 200; "S[tud?] H[orses?]": 0.

Tennessee Records of Grainger County-Tax Lists, 1797 [TN State Library and Archives]   FAMILY HISTORY LIBRARY film 464105

Glass, Major, Territory South of Ohio River, Blount County

Glass, Major,   Male

List, 21 Dec 1795, of members of Knoxville Convention.

Territorial Papers of the US - volume: 4 page: 415

Glass, Samuel, Territory South of Ohio River, Blount County

Glass, Samuel,   Male

On 3 Aug 1795 he was made First Major for Blount County.

Territorial Papers of the US - volume: 4 page: 469

Gordon, John, Territory South of Ohio River, Davidson County

Gordon, John,   Male

On 11 Jul 1795 he was made a Justice of the Peace for Davidson County.

Territorial Papers of the US - volume: 4 page: 468

Gray, Thomas, Esquire   Territory South of Ohio River

Gray, Thomas, Esquire Male **Job:** Attorney

On 7 Jan 1796 he was "licensed to practise law in the several Courts in the Territory."
Territorial Papers of the US - volume: 4 page: 471

Green, Daniel, Territory South of Ohio River, Hawkins County

Green, Daniel, Male

On 7 Feb 1795 he was made a Justice of the Peace for Hawkins County.
Territorial Papers of the US - volume: 4 page: 465

Greenaway, James, Territory South of Ohio River, Blount County

Greenaway, James, Male

List, 21 Dec 1795, of members of Knoxville Convention.
Territorial Papers of the US - volume: 4 page: 415

Greenaway, James, Territory South of Ohio River, Blount County

Greenaway, James, Male

On 3 Aug 1795 he was made a Justice of the Peace for Blount County.
Territorial Papers of the US - volume: 4 page: 469

Grubb, John, Tennessee, Grainger County

Grubb, John, Male

"Tax List Capt Jenings District taken in by Wm Hancock. 1797"; "W[hites?]": 1; "B[lacks?]": 0; "L[and?]": 300; "S[tud?] H[orses?]": 0.
Tennessee Records of Grainger County-Tax Lists, 1797 [TN State Library and Archives] FAMILY HISTORY LIBRARY film 464105

Guynn, Wm., Tennessee, Grainger County

Guynn, Wm., Male

"List of Taxable Property Harris Company Taken by James Moore. 1798"; Land: 200; "W[hite?] Pole": 1; "B[lack?] Pole": 0; "S[tud?] Horse": 0.
Tennessee Records of Grainger County-Tax Lists, 1798, [TN State Library and Archives] FAMILY HISTORY LIBRARY film 464105

Hains, John, Tennessee, Grainger County

Hains, John, Male

List of taxable property "Capt Margraves Compt 1799"; Lands: 100; "W[hite?] Poles": 0; "B[lack?] Poles": 0; "S[tud?] horses": 0; "Town Lots": 0.
Tennessee Records of Grainger County-Tax Lists, 1799, [TN State Library and Archives] FAMILY HISTORY LIBRARY film 464105

Hains, John, Tennessee, Grainger County

Hains, John, Male

"List of Taxable Property Harris Company Taken by James Moore. 1798"; Land: 100; "W[hite?] Pole": 0; "B[lack?] Pole": 0; "S[tud?] Horse": 0.
Page 33 is out of order and can be found on the microfilm following page 202. Page 33 has no heading, but the columns appear to be the same as those on page 32 and so will be considered as a part of that series. The entries appear to be crossed out.
Tennessee Records of Grainger County-Tax Lists, 1798, [TN State Library and Archives] FAMILY HISTORY LIBRARY film 464105

Hall, Joseph, Tennessee, Grainger County

Hall, Joseph, Male

List of taxable property "Capt Margraves Compt 1799"; Lands: 50; "W[hite?] Poles": 1; "B[lack?] Poles": 0; "S[tud?] horses": 0; "Town Lots": 0.
Tennessee Records of Grainger County-Tax Lists, 1799, [TN State Library and Archives] FAMILY HISTORY LIBRARY film 464105

Hall, William, Territory South of Ohio River, Sumner County

Hall, William, Male

On 1 Jan 1795 he was made an Ensign in the Regiment of Infantry for Sumner County.
Territorial Papers of the US - volume: 4 page: 464

Hall, William, Territory South of Ohio River, Sumner County

Hall, William, Male

On 6 Jul 1795 he was made Cornet of the Sumner Troop of Cavalry.
Territorial Papers of the US - volume: 4 page: 468

Hall?, John, Tennessee, Grainger County

Hall?, John, Male

"List of Taxable Property Harris Company Taken by James Moore. 1798"; Land: 200; "W[hite?] Pole": 1; "B[lack?] Pole": 0; "S[tud?] Horse": 0.
Tennessee Records of Grainger County-Tax Lists, 1798, [TN State Library and Archives] FAMILY HISTORY LIBRARY film 464105

Hamelton, William, Tennessee, Grainger County

Hamelton, William, Male

List of taxable property "Capt Margraves Compt 1799"; Lands: 400; "W[hite?] Poles": 0; "B[lack?] Poles": 0; "S[tud?] horses": 0; "Town Lots": 0.
Tennessee Records of Grainger County-Tax Lists, 1799, [TN State Library and Archives] FAMILY HISTORY LIBRARY film 464105

Hamock, Peter, Tennessee, Grainger County
Hamock, Peter, Male
"Tax List Capt Jenings District taken in by Wm Hancock. 1797"; "W[hites?]": 1; "B[lacks?]": 0; "L[and?]": 0; "S[tud?] H[orses?]": 0.
Tennessee Records of Grainger County-Tax Lists, 1797 [TN State Library and Archives]   FAMILY HISTORY LIBRARY film 464105
Hancock, Wm, Tennessee, Grainger County
Hancock, Wm, Male
"Tax List Capt Jenings District taken in by Wm Hancock. 1797"; "W[hites?]": 0; "B[lacks?]": 0; "L[and?]": 0; "S[tud?] H[orses?]": 0.
Tennessee Records of Grainger County-Tax Lists, 1797 [TN State Library and Archives]   FAMILY HISTORY LIBRARY film 464105
Hankins, William, Territory South of Ohio River, Sumner County
Hankins, William, Male
On 17 Jan 1795 he was made a Lieutenant in the Regiment of Infantry for Sumner County.
Territorial Papers of the US - volume: 4 page: 464
Hansborough, Smith, Territory South of Ohio River, Sumner County
Hansborough, Smith, Male
On 17 Jan 1795 he was made a Captain in the Regiment of Infantry for Sumner County.
Territorial Papers of the US - volume: 4 page: 464
Hardeman, Nicholas Perkins, Territory South of Ohio River, Davidson County
Hardeman, Nicholas Perkins, Male
On 27 Jan 1796 he was designated Collector "of the County and public taxes for the year 1796" for Davidson County.
Territorial Papers of the US - volume: 4 page: 471
Harden, Joseph, Territory South of Ohio River
Harden, Joseph, Male
"A native of Virginia and a citizen of Tyron County, Virginia, during the Revolution, in which he was an officer. Settled in Washington County, 1779; speaker of the Franklin Assembly, 1788, and of the second Territorial Assembly, 1795, [Williams, Lost State of Franklin,] pp. 297-298)."
Territorial Papers of the US - volume: 4 page: 435
Hardiman, Nicholas Perkins, Territory South of Ohio River, Davidson County
Hardiman, Nicholas Perkins, Male

On 14 Jul 1795 he was appointed Sheriff for Davidson County.
Territorial Papers of the US - volume: 4 page: 468
Hardiman, Nicholas Perkins, Territory South of Ohio River, Davidson County
Hardiman, Nicholas Perkins, Male
On 2 Feb 1795 he was appointed Sheriff and "Collector of the county and public taxes . . . in the Year 1795" for Davidson County.
Territorial Papers of the US - volume: 4 page: 465
Harmon, James, Tennessee, Grainger County
Harmon, James, Male
"List of Taxable Property Harris Company Taken by James Moore. 1798"; Land: 100; "W[hite?] Pole": 0; "B[lack?] Pole": 0; "S[tud?] Horse": 0.
Tennessee Records of Grainger County-Tax Lists, 1798, [TN State Library and Archives]   FAMILY HISTORY LIBRARY film 464105
Harmon, William, Tennessee, Grainger County
Harmon, William, Male
List of taxable property "Capt Margraves Compt 1799"; Lands: 200?; "W[hite?] Poles": 1; "B[lack?] Poles": 0; "S[tud?] horses": 0; "Town Lots": 0.
Tennessee Records of Grainger County-Tax Lists, 1799, [TN State Library and Archives]   FAMILY HISTORY LIBRARY film 464105
Harmon, William, Tennessee, Grainger County
Harmon, William, Male
"List of Taxable Property Harris Company Taken by James Moore. 1798"; Land: 119; "W[hite?] Pole": 1; "B[lack?] Pole": 0; "S[tud?] Horse": 0.
Page 33 is out of order and can be found on the microfilm following page 202. Page 33 has no heading, but the columns appear to be the same as those on page 32 and so will be considered as a part of that series. The entries appear to be crossed out.
Tennessee Records of Grainger County-Tax Lists, 1798, [TN State Library and Archives]   FAMILY HISTORY LIBRARY film 464105
Harris, , Tennessee, Grainger County
Harris, , Male
"List of Taxable Property Harris Company Taken by James Moore. 1798"; Land: 0; "W[hite?] Pole": 0; "B[lack?] Pole": 0; "S[tud?] Horse": 0.

Tennessee Records of Grainger County-Tax Lists, 1798, [TN State Library and Archives]   FAMILY HISTORY LIBRARY film 464105

Harris, Evin,   Tennessee, Grainger County

Harris, Evin,   Male

"List of Taxable Property Harris Company Taken by James Moore. 1798"; Land: 300; "W[hite?] Pole": 1; "B[lack?] Pole": 0; "S[tud?] Horse": 0.

Tennessee Records of Grainger County-Tax Lists, 1798, [TN State Library and Archives]   FAMILY HISTORY LIBRARY film 464105

Harris, Richard,   Tennessee, Grainger County

Harris, Richard,   Male

"Tax List Capt Jenings District taken in by Wm Hancock. 1797"; "W[hites?]": 1; "B[lacks?]": 0; "L[and?]": 0; "S[tud?] H[orses?]": 0.

Tennessee Records of Grainger County-Tax Lists, 1797 [TN State Library and Archives]   FAMILY HISTORY LIBRARY film 464105

Harris, Robert,   Tennessee, Grainger County

Harris, Robert,   Male

"List of Taxable Property Harris Company Taken by James Moore. 1798"; Land: 0; "W[hite?] Pole": 1; "B[lack?] Pole": 0; "S[tud?] Horse": 0.

Tennessee Records of Grainger County-Tax Lists, 1798, [TN State Library and Archives]   FAMILY HISTORY LIBRARY film 464105

Henderson, Robert,   Territory South of Ohio River, Sevier County

Henderson, Robert,   Male

On 7 Feb 1795 he was made a Cornet of the Sevier County Troop in the Regiment of Cavalry for Hamilton District.

Territorial Papers of the US - volume: 4 page: 466

Henderson, William,   Territory South of Ohio River, Sevier County

Henderson, William,   Male

On 7 Feb 1795 he was made a First Lieutenant of the Sevier County Troop in the Regiment of Cavalry for Hamilton District.

Territorial Papers of the US - volume: 4 page: 466

Hill, John,   Tennessee, Grainger County

Hill, John,   Male

"Tax List Capt Jenings District taken in by Wm Hancock. 1797"; "W[hites?]": 1; "B[lacks?]": 0; "L[and?]": 0; "S[tud?] H[orses?]": 0.

Hill, John,   Tennessee, Grainger County

Hill, John,   Male

"List of Taxable Property Harris Company Taken by James Moore. 1798"; Land: 0; "W[hite?] Pole": 0; "B[lack?] Pole": 1; "S[tud?] Horse": 0.

Tennessee Records of Grainger County-Tax Lists, 1798, [TN State Library and Archives]   FAMILY HISTORY LIBRARY film 464105

Hinsha, John,   Tennessee, Grainger County

Hinsha, John,   Male

"List of Taxable Property Harris Company Taken by James Moore. 1798"; Land: 200; "W[hite?] Pole": 1; "B[lack?] Pole": 0; "S[tud?] Horse": 0.

Tennessee Records of Grainger County-Tax Lists, 1798, [TN State Library and Archives]   FAMILY HISTORY LIBRARY film 464105

Hoalt, David, Sr   Tennessee, Grainger County

Hoalt, David, Sr   Male

"Tax List Capt Jenings District taken in by Wm Hancock. 1797"; "W[hites?]": 1; "B[lacks?]": 0; "L[and?]": 200; "S[tud?] H[orses?]": 0.

Tennessee Records of Grainger County-Tax Lists, 1797 [TN State Library and Archives]   FAMILY HISTORY LIBRARY film 464105

Hoalt, Edmon,   Tennessee, Grainger County

Hoalt, Edmon,   Male

"Tax List Capt Jenings District taken in by Wm Hancock. 1797"; "W[hites?]": 1; "B[lacks?]": 0; "L[and?]": 0; "S[tud?] H[orses?]": 0.

Tennessee Records of Grainger County-Tax Lists, 1797 [TN State Library and Archives]   FAMILY HISTORY LIBRARY film 464105

Hogan, Edward,   Territory South of Ohio River, Sumner County

Hogan, Edward,   Male

On 1 Jan 1795 he was made an Ensign in the Regiment of Infantry for Sumner County.

Territorial Papers of the US - volume: 4 page: 464

Holt, David, Jr.   Tennessee, Grainger County

Holt, David, Jr. Male

"Tax List Capt Jenings District taken in by Wm Hancock. 1797"; "W[hites?]": 1; "B[lacks?]": 0; "L[and?]": 0; "S[tud?] H[orses?]": 0.

Tennessee Records of Grainger County-Tax Lists,

1797 [TN State Library and Archives]   FAMILY HISTORY LIBRARY film 464105

Horver, John, Tennessee, Grainger County

Horver, John,   Male

"List of Taxable Property Harris Company Taken by James Moore. 1798"; Land: ?; "W[hite?] Pole": ?; "B[lack?] Pole": 0; "S[tud?] Horse": 0.

Tennessee Records of Grainger County-Tax Lists, 1798, [TN State Library and Archives]   FAMILY HISTORY LIBRARY film 464105

Houston, James,   Territory South of Ohio River, Blount County

Houston, James,   Male

On 3 Aug 1795 he was made an Ensign for Blount County.

Territorial Papers of the US - volume: 4 page: 469

Houston, James,   Territory South of Ohio River, Blount County

Houston, James,   Male

List, 21 Dec 1795, of members of Knoxville Convention.

Territorial Papers of the US - volume: 4 page: 415

Houston, Robert,   Territory South of Ohio River, Knox County

Houston, Robert,   Male

On 2 Feb 1795 he was appointed Sheriff and "Collector of the county and public taxes . . . in the Year 1795" for Knox County.

Territorial Papers of the US - volume: 4 page: 465

Houston, Robert,   Territory South of Ohio River, Knox County

Houston, Robert,   Male

On 27 Jan 1796 he was designated Collector "of the County and public taxes for the year 1796" for Knox County.

Territorial Papers of the US - volume: 4 page: 471

Houston, Robert,   Territory South of Ohio River, Knox County

Houston, Robert,   Male

On 2 May 1795 he was appointed Sheriff for Knox County.

Territorial Papers of the US - volume: 4 page: 467

Houston, Samuel,   Territory South of Ohio River, Blount County

Houston, Samuel,   Male

On 3 Aug 1795 he was made an Ensign for Blount County.

Territorial Papers of the US - volume: 4 page: 469

Houston, Samuel,   Territory South of Ohio River, Blount County

Houston, Samuel,   Male

On 3 Aug 1795 he was made a Justice of the Peace for Blount County.

Territorial Papers of the US - volume: 4 page: 469

Howth, William,   Tennessee, Grainger County

Howth, William,   Male

"Tax List Capt Jenings District taken in by Wm Hancock. 1797"; "W[hites?]": 1; "B[lacks?]": 0; "L[and?]": 140; "S[tud?] H[orses?]": 0.

Tennessee Records of Grainger County-Tax Lists, 1797 [TN State Library and Archives]   FAMILY HISTORY LIBRARY film 464105

Hubbard, James,   Territory South of Ohio River, Hamilton District

Hubbard, James,   Male

On 7 Feb 1795 he was made Second Major in the Regiment of Cavalry for Hamilton District.

Territorial Papers of the US - volume: 4 page: 466

Hunter, Frances,   Tennessee, Grainger County

Hunter, Frances,   Male

List of taxable property "Capt Margraves Compt 1799"; Lands: 100; "W[hite?] Poles": 0; "B[lack?] Poles": 0; "S[tud?] horses": 0; "Town Lots": 0.

Tennessee Records of Grainger County-Tax Lists, 1799, [TN State Library and Archives]   FAMILY HISTORY LIBRARY film 464105

Hunter, Mathew,   Tennessee, Grainger County

Hunter, Mathew,   Male

List of taxable property "Capt Margraves Compt 1799"; Lands: 100; "W[hite?] Poles": 0; "B[lack?] Poles": 0; "S[tud?] horses": 0; "Town Lots": 0.

Tennessee Records of Grainger County-Tax Lists, 1799, [TN State Library and Archives]   FAMILY HISTORY LIBRARY film 464105

Hunter, Robert,   Tennessee, Grainger County

Hunter, Robert, Male

"List of Taxable Property Harris Company Taken by James Moore. 1798"; Land: 800; "W[hite?] Pole": 0; "B[lack?] Pole": 0; "S[tud?] Horse": 0.

Tennessee Records of Grainger County-Tax Lists, 1798, [TN State Library and Archives]   FAMILY HISTORY LIBRARY film 464105

Hutcheson, Charles, Tennessee, Grainger County

Hutcheson, Charles,   Male

List of taxable property "Capt Margraves Compt 1799"; Lands: 140; "W[hite?] Poles": 1; "B[lack?] Poles": 2; "S[tud?] horses": 0; "Town Lots": 1.
Tennessee Records of Grainger County-Tax Lists, 1799, [TN State Library and Archives]   FAMILY HISTORY LIBRARY film 464105

Hutcheson, Charles,   Tennessee,   Grainger County

Hutcheson, Charles,   Male

He is listed in the bottom center of the page with no information given about him.
List of taxable property "Capt Margraves Compt 1799"; Lands: 0; "W[hite?] Poles": 0; "B[lack?] Poles": 0; "S[tud?] horses": 0; "Town Lots": 0.
Tennessee Records of Grainger County-Tax Lists, 1799, [TN State Library and Archives]   FAMILY HISTORY LIBRARY film 464105

Hutcheson, John,   Tennessee,   Grainger County

Hutcheson, John,   Male

List of taxable property "Capt Margraves Compt 1799"; Lands: 0; "W[hite?] Poles": 1; "B[lack?] Poles": 0; "S[tud?] horses": 0; "Town Lots": 0.
Tennessee Records of Grainger County-Tax Lists, 1799, [TN State Library and Archives]   FAMILY HISTORY LIBRARY film 464105

Hutcheson, Paul,   Tennessee,   Grainger County

Hutcheson, Paul,   Male

List of taxable property "Capt Margraves Compt 1799"; Lands: 50; "W[hite?] Poles": 0; "B[lack?] Poles": 0; "S[tud?] horses": 0; "Town Lots": 0.
Tennessee Records of Grainger County-Tax Lists, 1799, [TN State Library and Archives]   FAMILY HISTORY LIBRARY film 464105

Hutcheson, William,   Tennessee,   Grainger County

Hutcheson, William,   Male

List of taxable property "Capt Margraves Compt 1799"; Lands: 0; "W[hite?] Poles": 1; "B[lack?] Poles": 0; "S[tud?] horses": 0; "Town Lots": 0.
Tennessee Records of Grainger County-Tax Lists, 1799, [TN State Library and Archives]   FAMILY HISTORY LIBRARY film 464105

Inman, John,   Territory South of Ohio River, Jefferson County

Inman, John,   Male

On 8 Jul 1795 he was made a Captain in the Regiment of Infantry for Jefferson County.
Territorial Papers of the US - volume: 4 page: 468

Jackson, Forgerson,   Tennessee,   Grainger County

Jackson, Forgerson,   Male

List of taxable property "Capt Margraves Compt 1799"; Lands: 50; "W[hite?] Poles": 1; "B[lack?] Poles": 0; "S[tud?] horses": 0; "Town Lots": 0.
Tennessee Records of Grainger County-Tax Lists, 1799, [TN State Library and Archives]   FAMILY HISTORY LIBRARY film 464105

Jackson, Thomas,   Tennessee,   Grainger County

Jackson, Thomas,   Male

"List of Taxable Property Harris Company Taken by James Moore. 1798"; Land: 900; "W[hite?] Pole": 0; "B[lack?] Pole": 0; "S[tud?] Horse": 0.
Tennessee Records of Grainger County-Tax Lists, 1798, [TN State Library and Archives]   FAMILY HISTORY LIBRARY film 464105

James, William,   Tennessee,   Grainger County

James, William,   Male

"List of Taxable Property Harris Company Taken by James Moore. 1798"; Land: 50; "W[hite?] Pole": 0; "B[lack?] Pole": 2; "S[tud?] Horse": 0.
Page 33 is out of order and can be found on the microfilm following page 202. Page 33 has no heading, but the columns appear to be the same as those on page 32 and so will be considered as a part of that series. The entries appear to be crossed out.
Tennessee Records of Grainger County-Tax Lists, 1798, [TN State Library and Archives]   FAMILY HISTORY LIBRARY film 464105

James, William,   Tennessee,   Grainger County

James, William,   Male

List of taxable property "Capt Margraves Compt 1799"; Lands: 60; "W[hite?] Poles": 0; "B[lack?] Poles": 2; "S[tud?] horses": 0; "Town Lots": 0.
Tennessee Records of Grainger County-Tax Lists, 1799, [TN State Library and Archives]   FAMILY HISTORY LIBRARY film 464105

James, Wm, Jr.   Tennessee,   Grainger County

James, Wm, Jr. Male

"List of Taxable Property Harris Company Taken by James Moore. 1798"; Land: 0; "W[hite?] Pole": 1; "B[lack?] Pole": 0; "S[tud?] Horse": 0.
Tennessee Records of Grainger County-Tax Lists,

1798, [TN State Library and Archives] FAMILY HISTORY LIBRARY film 464105

Jarnagin, Noah, Tennessee, Grainger County

Jarnagin, Noah, Male

"List of Taxable Property Harris Company Taken by James Moore. 1798"; Land: 300; "W[hite?] Pole": 1; "B[lack?] Pole": 0; "S[tud?] Horse": 0.

Tennessee Records of Grainger County-Tax Lists, 1798, [TN State Library and Archives] FAMILY HISTORY LIBRARY film 464105

Jenings, , Capt Tennessee, Grainger County

Jenings, , Capt Male

"Tax List Capt Jenings District taken in by Wm Hancock. 1797"; "W[hites?]": 0; "B[lacks?]": 0; "L[and?]": 0; "S[tud?] H[orses?]": 0.

Tennessee Records of Grainger County-Tax Lists, 1797 [TN State Library and Archives] FAMILY HISTORY LIBRARY film 464105

Jennings, Jesse, Tennessee, Grainger County

Jennings, Jesse, Male

"List of Taxable Property Harris Company Taken by James Moore. 1798"; Land: 0; "W[hite?] Pole": 3; "B[lack?] Pole": 0; "S[tud?] Horse": 0.

Tennessee Records of Grainger County-Tax Lists, 1798, [TN State Library and Archives] FAMILY HISTORY LIBRARY film 464105

Johnson, Thomas, Territory South of Ohio River

Johnson, Thomas, Male

"Member of the constitutional convention, 1796, and of the second assembly of Tennessee (Moore, Hist. Tenn., I, 368)."

Territorial Papers of the US - volume: 4 page: 442

Jones, Peter, Tennessee, Grainger County

Jones, Peter, Male

"Tax List Capt Jenings District taken in by Wm Hancock. 1797"; "W[hites?]": 1; "B[lacks?]": 1; "L[and?]": 0; "S[tud?] H[orses?]": 0.

Tennessee Records of Grainger County-Tax Lists, 1797 [TN State Library and Archives] FAMILY HISTORY LIBRARY film 464105

Kellum, Daniel, Territory South of Ohio River, Hawkins County

Kellum, Daniel, Male

On 1 Aug 1795 he was made an Ensign in the militia for Hawkins County.

Territorial Papers of the US - volume: 4 page: 469

Kelly, Alexander, Territory South of Ohio River, Blount County

Kelly, Alexander, Male

On 3 Aug 1795 he was made Lieutenant Colonel Commandant for Blount County.

Territorial Papers of the US - volume: 4 page: 469

King, James, Territory South of Ohio River, Sullivan County

King, James, Male

On 11 Jul 1795 he was made a Justice of the Peace for Sullivan County.

Territorial Papers of the US - volume: 4 page: 468

Kitchen, John, Tennessee, Grainger County

Kitchen, John, Male

List of taxable property "Capt Margraves Compt 1799"; Lands: 0; "W[hite?] Poles": 1; "B[lack?] Poles": 0; "S[tud?] horses": 0; "Town Lots": 0.

Tennessee Records of Grainger County-Tax Lists, 1799, [TN State Library and Archives] FAMILY HISTORY LIBRARY film 464105

Lackey, James Woods, Territory South of Ohio River, Blount County

Lackey, James Woods, Male

On 3 Aug 1795 he was made Second Major for Blount County.

Territorial Papers of the US - volume: 4 page: 469

Laine, James, Tennessee, Grainger County

Laine, James, Male

List of taxable property "Capt Margraves Compt 1799"; Lands: 250; "W[hite?] Poles": 1; "B[lack?] Poles": 0; "S[tud?] horses": 0; "Town Lots": 0.

Tennessee Records of Grainger County-Tax Lists, 1799, [TN State Library and Archives] FAMILY HISTORY LIBRARY film 464105

Lamar, Young, Tennessee, Grainger County

Lamar, Young, Male

"List of Taxable Property Harris Company Taken by James Moore. 1798"; Land: 226; "W[hite?] Pole": 1; "B[lack?] Pole": 0; "S[tud?] Horse": 0.

Tennessee Records of Grainger County-Tax Lists, 1798, [TN State Library and Archives] FAMILY HISTORY LIBRARY film 464105

Latimer, , Territory South of Ohio River, Sumner County

Latimer, , Male

On 17 Jan 1795 he was made an Ensign in the Regiment of Infantry for Sumner County.

Territorial Papers of the US - volume: 4 page: 464

Lisby, Aaron, Tennessee, Grainger County

Lisby, Aaron,   Male
List of taxable property "Capt Margraves Compt 1799"; Lands: 200; "W[hite?] Poles": 0; "B[lack?] Poles": 0; "S[tud?] horses": 0; "Town Lots": 0.
Tennessee Records of Grainger County-Tax Lists, 1799, [TN State Library and Archives] FAMILY HISTORY LIBRARY film 464105
Long, Isaac,   Tennessee, Grainger County
        Long, Isaac,   Male
"Tax List Capt Jenings District taken in by Wm Hancock. 1797"; "W[hites?]": 1; "B[lacks?]": 0; "L[and?]": 40; "S[tud?] H[orses?]": 0.
Tennessee Records of Grainger County-Tax Lists, 1797 [TN State Library and Archives]   FAMILY HISTORY LIBRARY film 464105
Longacre, Benjamin, Territory South of Ohio River, Jefferson County
        Longacre, Benjamin,   Male
On 8 Jul 1795 he was made an Ensign in the Regiment of Infantry for Jefferson County.
Territorial Papers of the US - volume: 4 page: 468
Lovel, Jeremiah,   Tennessee,   Grainger County
        Lovel, Jeremiah,   Male
List of taxable property "Capt Margraves Compt 1799"; Lands: 0; "W[hite?] Poles": 1; "B[lack?] Poles": 0; "S[tud?] horses": 0; "Town Lots": 0.
Tennessee Records of Grainger County-Tax Lists, 1799, [TN State Library and Archives]   FAMILY HISTORY LIBRARY film 464105
Lowry, John, Territory South of Ohio River, Blount County
        Lowry, John,   Male
On 3 Aug 1795 he was made First Lieutenant in the Cavalry for Blount County.
Territorial Papers of the US - volume: 4 page: 469
Lowry, William,   Territory South of Ohio River, Blount County
        Lowry, William,   Male
On 3 Aug 1795 he was made a Justice of the Peace for Blount County.
Territorial Papers of the US - volume: 4 page: 469
Loyd, Owen,   Tennessee, Grainger County
        Loyd, Owen,   Male
"Tax List Capt Jenings District taken in by Wm Hancock. 1797"; "W[hites?]": 1; "B[lacks?]": 0; "L[and?]": 0; "S[tud?] H[orses?]": 0.
Tennessee Records of Grainger County-Tax Lists, 1797 [TN State Library and Archives]   FAMILY HISTORY LIBRARY film 464105

Lundy, Nathan,   Tennessee,   Grainger County
        Lundy, Nathan, Male
"Tax List Capt Jenings District taken in by Wm Hancock. 1797"; "W[hites?]": 1; "B[lacks?]": 0; "L[and?]": 0; "S[tud?] H[orses?]": 0.
Tennessee Records of Grainger County-Tax Lists, 1797 [TN State Library and Archives]   FAMILY HISTORY LIBRARY film 464105
M . . .?, Leny?,   Tennessee,   Grainger County
        M . . .?, Leny?, Male
        "Recorded at Leny[?] M . . .[?]" is written at the bottom center of the page.
List of taxable property "Capt Margraves Compt 1799"; Lands: 0; "W[hite?] Poles": 0; "B[lack?] Poles": 0; "S[tud?] horses": 0; "Town Lots": 0.
Tennessee Records of Grainger County-Tax Lists, 1799, [TN State Library and Archives]   FAMILY HISTORY LIBRARY film 464105
Mackenelly, Charles, Tennessee,   Grainger County
        Mackenelly, Charles,   Male
"Tax List Capt Jenings District taken in by Wm Hancock. 1797"; "W[hites?]": 1; "B[lacks?]": 0; "L[and?]": 0; "S[tud?] H[orses?]": 0.
Tennessee Records of Grainger County-Tax Lists, 1797 [TN State Library and Archives]   FAMILY HISTORY LIBRARY film 464105
Maclin, Robert,   Territory South of Ohio River, Washington County
        Maclin, Robert,   Male
On 6 Feb 1796 he was made a Justice of the Peace for Washington County.
Territorial Papers of the US - volume: 4 page: 471
Marcy, Jonathan,   Tennessee,   Grainger County
        Marcy, Jonathan,   Male
"List of Taxable Property Harris Company Taken by James Moore. 1798"; Land: 0; "W[hite?] Pole": 1; "B[lack?] Pole": 0; "S[tud?] Horse": 0.
Tennessee Records of Grainger County-Tax Lists, 1798, [TN State Library and Archives]   FAMILY HISTORY LIBRARY film 464105
Margrave, , Capt   Tennessee,   Grainger County
        Margrave, , Capt   Male
List of taxable property "Capt Margraves Compt 1799"; Lands: 0; "W[hite?] Poles": 0; "B[lack?] Poles": 0; "S[tud?] horses": 0; "Town Lots": 0.

Tennessee Records of Grainger County-Tax Lists, 1799, [TN State Library and Archives] FAMILY HISTORY LIBRARY film 464105

Masingale, Michael, Tennessee, Grainger County

Masingale, Michael, Male

"List of Taxable Property Harris Company Taken by James Moore. 1798"; Land: 200; "W[hite?] Pole": 1; "B[lack?] Pole": 0; "S[tud?] Horse": 0.

Tennessee Records of Grainger County-Tax Lists, 1798, [TN State Library and Archives] FAMILY HISTORY LIBRARY film 464105

Massingale, William, Territory South of Ohio River, Sevier County

Massingale, William, Male

On 7 Feb 1795 he was made a Second Lieutenant of the Sevier County Troop in the Regiment of Cavalry for Hamilton District.

Territorial Papers of the US - volume: 4 page: 466

Matlock, John, Tennessee, Grainger County

Matlock, John, Male

"List of Taxable Property Harris Company Taken by James Moore. 1798"; Land: 300; "W[hite?] Pole": 1; "B[lack?] Pole": 0; "S[tud?] Horse": 0.

Tennessee Records of Grainger County-Tax Lists, 1798, [TN State Library and Archives] FAMILY HISTORY LIBRARY film 464105

Maxfield, Seth, Tennessee, Grainger County

Maxfield, Seth, Male

"List of Taxable Property Harris Company Taken by James Moore. 1798"; Land: 200; "W[hite?] Pole": 1; "B[lack?] Pole": 0; "S[tud?] Horse": 0.

Tennessee Records of Grainger County-Tax Lists, 1798, [TN State Library and Archives] FAMILY HISTORY LIBRARY film 464105

Maxwell, George, Territory South of Ohio River, Hawkins County

Maxwell, George, Male

"A native of Virginia; appointed justice of Sullivan County on its first organization; representative in the North Carolina Assembly, 1787-1788; colonel of militia, 1788; representative from Hawkins County in the Tennessee Senate, 1799 (Williams, op. cit., pp. 328-329)."

Territorial Papers of the US - volume: 4 page: 433

McAlpin, Alexander, Territory South of Ohio River, Washington District

McAlpin, Alexander, Male

On 27 Nov 1795 he was "appointed Cornet of Cavalry in the Regiment of Washington District."

Territorial Papers of the US - volume: 4 page: 470

McCarty, Benjamin, Territory South of Ohio River, Hawkins County

McCarty, Benjamin, Male

On 25 Jan 1796 he was made a Justice of the Peace for Hawkins County.

Territorial Papers of the US - volume: 4 page: 471

McClellan, John, Territory South of Ohio River, Knox County

McClellan, John, Male

On 26 Nov 1795 he was made a Justice of the Peace for Knox County.

Territorial Papers of the US - volume: 4 page: 470

McClellan, John, Territory South of Ohio River, Hamilton District

McClellan, John, Male

On 27 Jan 1795 he was made a Captain in the Regiment of Cavalry for Hamilton District.

Territorial Papers of the US - volume: 4 page: 464

McClellan, Samuel, Territory South of Ohio River, Hamilton District

McClellan, Samuel, Male

On 2 Aug 1795 he was made First Lieutenant in the Cavalry for Hamilton District.

Territorial Papers of the US - volume: 4 page: 469

McClellan, Samuel, Territory South of Ohio River, Hamilton District

McClellan, Samuel, Male

On 7 Feb 1795 he was made a Second Lieutenant in the Regiment of Cavalry for Hamilton District.

Territorial Papers of the US - volume: 4 page: 465

McClung, Charles, Territory South of Ohio River, Hamilton District

McClung, Charles, Male

On 2 Aug 1795 he was made Second Lieutenant in the Cavalry for Hamilton District.

Territorial Papers of the US - volume: 4 page: 469

McClung, Charles, Territory South of Ohio River, Hamilton District

McClung, Charles, Male

On 7 Feb 1795 he was made a Cornet in the Regiment of Cavalry for Hamilton District.

Territorial Papers of the US - volume: 4 page: 465

McClung, Charles, Territory South of Ohio River, Knox County

McClung, Charles, Male

List, 21 Dec 1795, of members of Knoxville Convention.

Territorial Papers of the US - volume: 4 page: 415
McCoy, Moses, Territory South of Ohio River, Jefferson County
McCoy, Moses, Male
On 8 Jul 1795 he was made a Lieutenant in the Regiment of Infantry for Jefferson County.
Territorial Papers of the US - volume: 4 page: 468
McCulloch, Thomas, Territory South of Ohio River, Blount County
McCulloch, Thomas, Male
On 3 Aug 1795 he was made a Justice of the Peace for Blount County.
Territorial Papers of the US - volume: 4 page: 469
McElwrath, Joseph, Territory South of Ohio River, Sumner County
McElwrath, Joseph, Male
On 17 Jan 1795 he was made Second Major in the Regiment of Infantry for Sumner County.
Territorial Papers of the US - volume: 4 page: 464
McFarlan, Robert, Territory South of Ohio River, Jefferson County
McFarlan, Robert, Male
On 2 Feb 1795 he was appointed Sheriff and "Collector of the county and public taxes . . . in the Year 1795" for Jefferson County.
Territorial Papers of the US - volume: 4 page: 465
Mcfarland, George, Territory South of Ohio River, Jefferson County
Mcfarland, George, Male
On 8 Jul 1795 he was made a Lieutenant in the Regiment of Infantry for Jefferson County.
Territorial Papers of the US - volume: 4 page: 468
Mcfarland, Robert, Territory South of Ohio River, Jefferson County
Mcfarland, Robert, Male
On 27 Jan 1796 he was designated Collector "of the County and public taxes for the year 1796" for Jefferson County.
Territorial Papers of the US - volume: 4 page: 471
McKee, John, Territory South of Ohio River, Blount County
McKee, John, Male
On 3 Aug 1795 he was made Lieutenant Colonel for Blount County.
Territorial Papers of the US - volume: 4 page: 469
McKee, John, Territory South of Ohio River
McKee, John, Male **Job:** Attorney
On 28 Jan 1795 he was licensed to "practise as an Attorney in the Court of Pleas and Quarter Sessions."

Territorial Papers of the US - volume: 4 page: 464
McKee, John, Territory South of Ohio River, Blount County
McKee, John, Male
On 3 Aug 1795 he was made Clerk for Blount County.
Territorial Papers of the US - volume: 4 page: 469
McNutt, Isaac, Territory South of Ohio River
McNutt, Isaac, Male **Job:** Attorney
On 23 Oct 1795 he was "licensed to practise as an Attorney at Law, in the several County Courts."
Territorial Papers of the US - volume: 4 page: 469
McPhetridge, William, Tennessee, Grainger County
McPhetridge, William, Male
List of taxable property "Capt Margraves Compt 1799"; Lands: 100; "W[hite?] Poles": 1; "B[lack?] Poles": 0; "S[tud?] horses": 0; "Town Lots": 0.
Tennessee Records of Grainger County-Tax Lists, 1799, [TN State Library and Archives] FAMILY HISTORY LIBRARY film 464105
McQueston, James, Territory South of Ohio River, Jefferson County
McQueston, James, Male
On 8 Jul 1795 he was made a Lieutenant in the Regiment of Infantry for Jefferson County.
Territorial Papers of the US - volume: 4 page: 468
Medley, James, Tennessee, Grainger County
Medley, James, Male
List of taxable property "Capt Margraves Compt 1799"; Lands: 0; "W[hite?] Poles": 1; "B[lack?] Poles": 0; "S[tud?] horses": 0; "Town Lots": 0.
Tennessee Records of Grainger County-Tax Lists, 1799, [TN State Library and Archives] FAMILY HISTORY LIBRARY film 464105
Merriot, John, Tennessee, Grainger County
Merriot, John, Male
"List of Taxable Property Harris Company Taken by James Moore. 1798"; Land: 200; "W[hite?] Pole": 1; "B[lack?] Pole": 0; "S[tud?] Horse": 0.
Tennessee Records of Grainger County-Tax Lists, 1798, [TN State Library and Archives] FAMILY HISTORY LIBRARY film 464105
Miles, William, Territory South of Ohio River, Tennessee County
Miles, William, Male
On 14 Jul 1795 he was made Second Major of the Infantry for Tennessee County.

Territorial Papers of the US - volume: 4 page: 468
Miller, George, Tennessee, Grainger County
Miller, George, Male
"List of Taxable Property Harris Company Taken by James Moore. 1798"; Land: 0; "W[hite?] Pole": 1; "B[lack?] Pole": 0; "S[tud?] Horse": 0.
Tennessee Records of Grainger County-Tax Lists, 1798, [TN State Library and Archives] FAMILY HISTORY LIBRARY film 464105
Miller, Martin, Tennessee, Grainger County
Miller, Martin, Male
"List of Taxable Property Harris Company Taken by James Moore. 1798"; Land: 150; "W[hite?] Pole": 1; "B[lack?] Pole": 0; "S[tud?] Horse": 0.
Tennessee Records of Grainger County-Tax Lists, 1798, [TN State Library and Archives] FAMILY HISTORY LIBRARY film 464105
Moor, Abner, Tennessee, Grainger County
Moor, Abner, Male
"Tax List Capt Jenings District taken in by Wm Hancock. 1797"; "W[hites?]": 1; "B[lacks?]": 0; "L[and?]": 100; "S[tud?] H[orses?]": 0.
Tennessee Records of Grainger County-Tax Lists, 1797 [TN State Library and Archives] FAMILY HISTORY LIBRARY film 464105
Moor, Rubin, Tennessee, Grainger County
Moor, Rubin, Male
"Tax List Capt Jenings District taken in by Wm Hancock. 1797"; "W[hites?]": 1; "B[lacks?]": 0; "L[and?]": 0; "S[tud?] H[orses?]": 0.
Tennessee Records of Grainger County-Tax Lists, 1797 [TN State Library and Archives] FAMILY HISTORY LIBRARY film 464105
Moore, James, Tennessee, Grainger County
Moore, James, Male
"List of Taxable Property Harris Company Taken by James Moore. 1798"; Land: 382; "W[hite?] Pole": 1; "B[lack?] Pole": 0; "S[tud?] Horse": 0.
Tennessee Records of Grainger County-Tax Lists, 1798, [TN State Library and Archives] FAMILY HISTORY LIBRARY film 464105
Moore, James, Tennessee, Grainger County
Moore, James, Male
"List of Taxable Property Harris Company Taken by James Moore. 1798"; Land: 0; "W[hite?] Pole": 0; "B[lack?] Pole": 0; "S[tud?] Horse": 0.

Tennessee Records of Grainger County-Tax Lists, 1798, [TN State Library and Archives] FAMILY HISTORY LIBRARY film 464105
Moore?, [Unreadable], Tennessee, Grainger County
Moore?, [Unreadable], Male
"List of Taxable Property Harris Company Taken by James Moore. 1798"; Land: 330; "W[hite?] Pole": 1; "B[lack?] Pole": 0; "S[tud?] Horse": 0.
Tennessee Records of Grainger County-Tax Lists, 1798, [TN State Library and Archives] FAMILY HISTORY LIBRARY film 464105
Morrow, Alexd, Tennessee, Grainger County
Morrow, Alexd, Male
"List of Taxable Property Harris Company Taken by James Moore. 1798"; Land: 320; "W[hite?] Pole": 1; "B[lack?] Pole": 0; "S[tud?] Horse": 0.
Tennessee Records of Grainger County-Tax Lists, 1798, [TN State Library and Archives] FAMILY HISTORY LIBRARY film 464105
Moyars, James, Territory South of Ohio River, Jefferson County
Moyars, James, Male
On 8 Jul 1795 he was made a Lieutenant in the Regiment of Infantry for Jefferson County.
Territorial Papers of the US - volume: 4 page: 468
Moyrs, John, Tennessee, Grainger County
Moyrs, John, Male
"Tax List Capt Jenings District taken in by Wm Hancock. 1797"; "W[hites?]": 1; "B[lacks?]": 0; "L[and?]": 100; "S[tud?] H[orses?]": 0.
Tennessee Records of Grainger County-Tax Lists, 1797 [TN State Library and Archives] FAMILY HISTORY LIBRARY film 464105
Murphy, Wm, Tennessee, Grainger County
Murphy, Wm, Male
"List of Taxable Property Harris Company Taken by James Moore. 1798"; Land: 0; "W[hite?] Pole": 1; "B[lack?] Pole": 0; "S[tud?] Horse": 0.
Tennessee Records of Grainger County-Tax Lists, 1798, [TN State Library and Archives] FAMILY HISTORY LIBRARY film 464105
Murray, Thomas, Territory South of Ohio River, Davidson County
Murray, Thomas, Male
On 8 Jul 1795 he was made First Major for Davidson County.
Territorial Papers of the US - volume: 4 page: 468

Nelson, William, Territory South of Ohio River, Washington County

Nelson, William, Male

On 11 Jul 1795 he was made a Justice of the Peace for Washington County.

Territorial Papers of the US - volume: 4 page: 468

Nevill, Joseph, Territory South of Ohio River, Tennessee County

Nevill, Joseph, Male

On 14 Jul 1795 he was appointed Sheriff for Tennessee County.

Territorial Papers of the US - volume: 4 page: 468

Nevill, Joseph B., Territory South of Ohio River, Tennessee County

Nevill, Joseph B., Male

On 27 Jan 1796 he was designated Collector "of the County and public taxes for the year 1796" for Tennessee County.

Territorial Papers of the US - volume: 4 page: 471

Neville, Joseph, Territory South of Ohio River, Tennessee County

Neville, Joseph, Male

On 2 Feb 1795 he was appointed Sheriff and "Collector of the county and public taxes . . . in the Year 1795" for Tennessee County.

Territorial Papers of the US - volume: 4 page: 465

Norris, Garit, Tennessee, Grainger County

Norris, Garit, Male

List of taxable property "Capt Margraves Compt 1799"; Lands: 50; "W[hite?] Poles": 1; "B[lack?] Poles": 0; "S[tud?] horses": 0; "Town Lots": 0.

Tennessee Records of Grainger County-Tax Lists, 1799, [TN State Library and Archives] FAMILY HISTORY LIBRARY film 464105

Norris, Gorge, Tennessee, Grainger County

Norris, Gorge, Male

List of taxable property "Capt Margraves Compt 1799"; Lands: 165; "W[hite?] Poles": 1; "B[lack?] Poles": 0; "S[tud?] horses": 0; "Town Lots": 0.

Tennessee Records of Grainger County-Tax Lists, 1799, [TN State Library and Archives] FAMILY HISTORY LIBRARY film 464105

Norris, Jeremiah, Tennessee, Grainger County

Norris, Jeremiah, Male

List of taxable property "Capt Margraves Compt 1799"; Lands: 0; "W[hite?] Poles": 1; "B[lack?] Poles": 0; "S[tud?] horses": 0; "Town Lots": 0.

Tennessee Records of Grainger County-Tax Lists, 1799, [TN State Library and Archives] FAMILY HISTORY LIBRARY film 464105

Norris, William, Tennessee, Grainger County

Norris, William, Male

List of taxable property "Capt Margraves Compt 1799"; Lands: 250; "W[hite?] Poles": 0; "B[lack?] Poles": 0; "S[tud?] horses": 0; "Town Lots": 0.

Tennessee Records of Grainger County-Tax Lists, 1799, [TN State Library and Archives] FAMILY HISTORY LIBRARY film 464105

Norris, William, Jr. Tennessee, Grainger County

Norris, William, Jr. Male

List of taxable property "Capt Margraves Compt 1799"; Lands: 0; "W[hite?] Poles": 1; "B[lack?] Poles": 0; "S[tud?] horses": 0; "Town Lots": 0.

Tennessee Records of Grainger County-Tax Lists, 1799, [TN State Library and Archives] FAMILY HISTORY LIBRARY film 464105

Outlaw, , Col: Territory South of Ohio River, Jefferson County

Outlaw, , Col: Male

List, 21 Dec 1795, of members of Knoxville Convention.

Territorial Papers of the US - volume: 4 page: 415

Outlaw, Alexander, Territory South of Ohio River

Outlaw, Alexander, Male

"A native of North Carolina, removing to Greene (now Jefferson) County, in 1783; a participant in the Franklin movement; a member of the Tennessee constitutional convention, 1796, and a representative in the first State Assembly. He was the father-in-law of Judges David Campbell and Joseph Anderson, [(Williams, Lost State of Franklin,] pp. 316-318)."

Territorial Papers of the US - volume: 4 page: 435

Owens, John, Tennessee, Grainger County

Owens, John, Male

"List of Taxable Property Harris Company Taken by James Moore. 1798"; Land: 0; "W[hite?] Pole": 1; "B[lack?] Pole": 0; "S[tud?] Horse": 0.

Tennessee Records of Grainger County-Tax Lists, 1798, [TN State Library and Archives] FAMILY HISTORY LIBRARY film 464105

Parker, Isham Allen, Territory South of Ohio River

Parker, Isham Allen,   Male   **Job: Attorney**
On 24 Oct 1795 he was "licensed to practise as an Attorney in the several county courts of pleas and Quarter Sessions."
Territorial Papers of the US - volume: 4 page: 470
Parker, James,   Tennessee,   Grainger County
          Parker, James,   Male
"List of Taxable Property Harris Company Taken by James Moore. 1798"; Land: 410; "W[hite?] Pole": 1; "B[lack?] Pole": 0; "S[tud?] Horse": 0.
Page 33 is out of order and can be found on the microfilm following page 202. Page 33 has no heading, but the columns appear to be the same as those on page 32 and so will be considered as a part of that series. The entries appear to be crossed out.
Tennessee Records of Grainger County-Tax Lists, 1798, [TN State Library and Archives]   FAMILY HISTORY LIBRARY film 464105
Parker, Philip,   Tennessee,   Grainger County
          Parker, Philip,   Male
"List of Taxable Property Harris Company Taken by James Moore. 1798"; Land: 0; "W[hite?] Pole": 1; "B[lack?] Pole": 0; "S[tud?] Horse": 0.
Page 33 is out of order and can be found on the microfilm following page 202. Page 33 has no heading, but the columns appear to be the same as those on page 32 and so will be considered as a part of that series. The entries appear to be crossed out.
Tennessee Records of Grainger County-Tax Lists, 1798, [TN State Library and Archives]   FAMILY HISTORY LIBRARY film 464105
Parker, Phillip,   Tennessee,   Grainger County
          Parker, Phillip, Male
List of taxable property "Capt Margraves Compt 1799"; Lands: 30; "W[hite?] Poles": 1; "B[lack?] Poles": 0; "S[tud?] horses": 0; "Town Lots": 0.
Tennessee Records of Grainger County-Tax Lists, 1799, [TN State Library and Archives]   FAMILY HISTORY LIBRARY film 464105
Patterson, Robert,   Territory South of Ohio River, Knox County
          Patterson, Robert,   Male
On 26 Nov 1795 he was made a Lieutenant in the Knox Regiment.

Territorial Papers of the US - volume: 4 page: 470
Peters, Jasuaway,   Tennessee,   Grainger County
          Peters, Jasuaway,   Male
List of taxable property "Capt Margraves Compt 1799"; Lands: 0; "W[hite?] Poles": 1; "B[lack?] Poles": 0; "S[tud?] horses": 0; "Town Lots": 0.
Tennessee Records of Grainger County-Tax Lists, 1799, [TN State Library and Archives]   FAMILY HISTORY LIBRARY film 464105
Peters, John,   Tennessee, Grainger County
          Peters, John,   Male
List of taxable property "Capt Margraves Compt 1799"; Lands: 260; "W[hite?] Poles": 1; "B[lack?] Poles": 0; "S[tud?] horses": 0; "Town Lots": 0.
Tennessee Records of Grainger County-Tax Lists, 1799, [TN State Library and Archives]   FAMILY HISTORY LIBRARY film 464105
Peters, Joseph,   Tennessee,   Grainger County
          Peters, Joseph,   Male
List of taxable property "Capt Margraves Compt 1799"; Lands: 0; "W[hite?] Poles": 1; "B[lack?] Poles": 0; "S[tud?] horses": 0; "Town Lots": 0.
Tennessee Records of Grainger County-Tax Lists, 1799, [TN State Library and Archives]   FAMILY HISTORY LIBRARY film 464105
Peters, Nathaniel,   Tennessee,   Grainger County
          Peters, Nathaniel,   Male
List of taxable property "Capt Margraves Compt 1799"; Lands: 360; "W[hite?] Poles": 0; "B[lack?] Poles": 0; "S[tud?] horses": 0; "Town Lots": 0.
Tennessee Records of Grainger County-Tax Lists, 1799, [TN State Library and Archives]   FAMILY HISTORY LIBRARY film 464105
Peters, William,   Tennessee,   Grainger County
          Peters, William,   Male
List of taxable property "Capt Margraves Compt 1799"; Lands: 275; "W[hite?] Poles": 1; "B[lack?] Poles": 0; "S[tud?] horses": 0; "Town Lots": 0.
Tennessee Records of Grainger County-Tax Lists, 1799, [TN State Library and Archives]   FAMILY HISTORY LIBRARY film 464105
Petre, Adam,   Tennessee, Grainger County
          Petre, Adam,   Male
"Tax List Capt Jenings District taken in by Wm Hancock. 1797"; "W[hites?]": 1; "B[lacks?]": 0; "L[and?]": 0; "S[tud?] H[orses?]": 0.

Tennessee Records of Grainger County-Tax Lists, 1797 [TN State Library and Archives]   FAMILY HISTORY LIBRARY film 464105

Petre, George, Tennessee, Grainger County

Petre, George,   Male

"Tax List Capt Jenings District taken in by Wm Hancock. 1797"; "W[hites?]": 1; "B[lacks?]": 0; "L[and?]": 200; "S[tud?] H[orses?]": 0.

Tennessee Records of Grainger County-Tax Lists, 1797 [TN State Library and Archives]   FAMILY HISTORY LIBRARY film 464105

Petre, John,   Tennessee, Grainger County

Petre, John,   Male

"Tax List Capt Jenings District taken in by Wm Hancock. 1797"; "W[hites?]": 1; "B[lacks?]": 0; "L[and?]": 0; "S[tud?] H[orses?]": 0.

Tennessee Records of Grainger County-Tax Lists, 1797 [TN State Library and Archives]   FAMILY HISTORY LIBRARY film 464105

Presgrove, Barnabas, Tennessee,   Grainger County

Presgrove, Barnabas,   Male

"List of Taxable Property Harris Company Taken by James Moore. 1798"; Land: 50; "W[hite?] Pole": 1; "B[lack?] Pole": 0; "S[tud?] Horse": 0.

Tennessee Records of Grainger County-Tax Lists, 1798, [TN State Library and Archives]   FAMILY HISTORY LIBRARY film 464105

Presgrove, George,   Tennessee,   Grainger County

Presgrove, George,   Male

"List of Taxable Property Harris Company Taken by James Moore. 1798"; Land: 0; "W[hite?] Pole": 1; "B[lack?] Pole": 0; "S[tud?] Horse": 0.

Tennessee Records of Grainger County-Tax Lists, 1798, [TN State Library and Archives]   FAMILY HISTORY LIBRARY film 464105

Pruett, Abraham,   Tennessee,   Grainger County

Pruett, Abraham,   Male

"Tax List Capt Jenings District taken in by Wm Hancock. 1797"; "W[hites?]": 1; "B[lacks?]": 0; "L[and?]": 0; "S[tud?] H[orses?]": 0.

Tennessee Records of Grainger County-Tax Lists, 1797 [TN State Library and Archives]   FAMILY HISTORY LIBRARY film 464105

Ragan, Henry, Territory South of Ohio River, Blount County

Ragan, Henry,   Male

On 3 Aug 1795 he was made an Ensign for Blount County.

Territorial Papers of the US - volume: 4 page: 469

Ragan, John, Territory South of Ohio River, Blount County

Ragan, John,   Male

On 3 Aug 1795 he was made an Ensign for Blount County.

Territorial Papers of the US - volume: 4 page: 469

Ragan, William,   Territory South of Ohio River, Blount County

Ragan, William,   Male

On 3 Aug 1795 he was made a Lieutenant for Blount County.

Territorial Papers of the US - volume: 4 page: 469

Ragen, Henry, Territory South of Ohio River, Knox County

Ragen, Henry,   Male

On 3 Feb 1795 he was made an Ensign in the Knox Regiment of Infantry.

Territorial Papers of the US - volume: 4 page: 465

Ramsey, Samuel,   Tennessee,   Grainger County

Ramsey, Samuel,   Male

"Tax List Capt Jenings District taken in by Wm Hancock. 1797"; "W[hites?]": 1; "B[lacks?]": 0; "L[and?]": 0; "S[tud?] H[orses?]": 0.

Tennessee Records of Grainger County-Tax Lists, 1797 [TN State Library and Archives]   FAMILY HISTORY LIBRARY film 464105

Ray, Joseph,   Tennessee, Grainger County

Ray, Joseph,   Male

"List of Taxable Property Harris Company Taken by James Moore. 1798"; Land: 0; "W[hite?] Pole": 1; "B[lack?] Pole": 0; "S[tud?] Horse": 0.

Tennessee Records of Grainger County-Tax Lists, 1798, [TN State Library and Archives]   FAMILY HISTORY LIBRARY film 464105

Reed, Thomas,   Tennessee,   Grainger County

Reed, Thomas, Male

"List of Taxable Property Harris Company Taken by James Moore. 1798"; Land: 355; "W[hite?] Pole": 1; "B[lack?] Pole": 0; "S[tud?] Horse": 0.

Tennessee Records of Grainger County-Tax Lists, 1798, [TN State Library and Archives]   FAMILY HISTORY LIBRARY film 464105

Renno, William,   Territory South of Ohio River, Sevier County

Renno, William,   Male

On 15 Jul 1795 he was made a Justice of the Peace for Sevier County.
Territorial Papers of the US - volume: 4 page: 468
Rhea, Matthew, Territory South of Ohio River, Sullivan County
Rhea, Matthew, Male
On 31 Jan 1795 he was appointed Lieutenant Colonel of the Sullivan Regiment of Infantry.
Territorial Papers of the US - volume: 4 page: 465
Rhea, Robert, Territory South of Ohio River, Blount County
Rhea, Robert, Male
On 3 Aug 1795 he was made Coroner for Blount County.
Territorial Papers of the US - volume: 4 page: 469
Rhea, Robert, Territory South of Ohio River, Blount County
Rhea, Robert, Male
On 3 Aug 1795 he was made an Ensign for Blount County.
Territorial Papers of the US - volume: 4 page: 469
Rice, Henry, Tennessee, Grainger County
Rice, Henry, Male
"List of Taxable Property Harris Company Taken by James Moore. 1798"; Land: 420; "W[hite?] Pole": 0; "B[lack?] Pole": 0; "S[tud?] Horse": 0.
Tennessee Records of Grainger County-Tax Lists, 1798, [TN State Library and Archives] FAMILY HISTORY LIBRARY film 464105
Rice, James, Tennessee, Grainger County
Rice, James, Male
"List of Taxable Property Harris Company Taken by James Moore. 1798"; Land: 0; "W[hite?] Pole": 1; "B[lack?] Pole": 0; "S[tud?] Horse": 0.
Tennessee Records of Grainger County-Tax Lists, 1798, [TN State Library and Archives] FAMILY HISTORY LIBRARY film 464105
Richardson, James, Tennessee, Grainger County
Richardson, James, Male
"List of Taxable Property Harris Company Taken by James Moore. 1798"; Land: 490; "W[hite?] Pole": 1; "B[lack?] Pole": 0; "S[tud?] Horse": 0.
Tennessee Records of Grainger County-Tax Lists, 1798, [TN State Library and Archives] FAMILY HISTORY LIBRARY film 464105
Roaks, Aaron, Tennessee, Grainger County
Roaks, Aaron, Male

"Tax List Capt Jenings District taken in by Wm Hancock. 1797"; "W[hites?]": 1; "B[lacks?]": 0; "L[and?]": 0; "S[tud?] H[orses?]": 0.
Tennessee Records of Grainger County-Tax Lists, 1797 [TN State Library and Archives] FAMILY HISTORY LIBRARY film 464105
Roan, Archibald, Territory South of Ohio River, Jefferson County
Roan, Archibald, Male **Job:** "a lawyer"
List, 21 Dec 1795, of members of Knoxville Convention.
Territorial Papers of the US - volume: 4 page: 415
Roberts, Henry, Territory South of Ohio River, Hamilton District
Roberts, Henry, Male
On 2 Aug 1795 he was made Cornet in the Cavalry for Hamilton District.
Territorial Papers of the US - volume: 4 page: 469
Roddy, , Col: Territory South of Ohio River, Jefferson County
Roddy, , Col: Male
List, 21 Dec 1795, of members of Knoxville Convention.
Territorial Papers of the US - volume: 4 page: 415
Rogers, George, Territory South of Ohio River, Jefferson County
Rogers, George, Male
On 8 Jul 1795 he was made an Ensign in the Regiment of Infantry for Jefferson County.
Territorial Papers of the US - volume: 4 page: 468
Russell, William, Tennessee, Grainger County
Russell, William, Male
"List of Taxable Property Harris Company Taken by James Moore. 1798"; Land: 200; "W[hite?] Pole": 1; "B[lack?] Pole": 0; "S[tud?] Horse": 0.
Tennessee Records of Grainger County-Tax Lists, 1798, [TN State Library and Archives] FAMILY HISTORY LIBRARY film 464105
Rutledge, George, Territory South of Ohio River, Sullivan County
Rutledge, George, Male
On 31 Jan 1795 he was made a Justice of the Peace for Sullivan County.
Territorial Papers of the US - volume: 4 page: 465
Rutledge, George, Territory South of Ohio River, Sullivan County
Rutledge, George, Male

On 31 Jan 1795 he was appointed First Major of the Sullivan Regiment of Infantry.
Territorial Papers of the US - volume: 4 page: 465
Scott, James, Territory South of Ohio River, Blount County
Scott, James, Male
On 3 Aug 1795 he was made an Ensign for Blount County.
Territorial Papers of the US - volume: 4 page: 469
Scott, James, Territory South of Ohio River, Blount County
Scott, James, Male
On 3 Aug 1795 he was made a Justice of the Peace for Blount County.
Territorial Papers of the US - volume: 4 page: 469
Scott, John, Territory South of Ohio River, Sullivan County?
Scott, John, Male
On 31 Jan 1795 he was appointed Lieutenant Colonel Commandant [of the Sullivan Regiment of Infantry?]
Territorial Papers of the US - volume: 4 page: 465
Scott, John, Territory South of Ohio River, Sullivan County
Scott, John, Male
On 2 Feb 1795 he was appointed Sheriff and "Collector of the county and public taxes . . . in the Year 1795" for Sullivan County.
Territorial Papers of the US - volume: 4 page: 465
Selvage, Jeremiah, Tennessee, Grainger County
Selvage, Jeremiah, Male
List of taxable property "Capt Margraves Compt 1799"; Lands: 0; "W[hite?] Poles": 1; "B[lack?] Poles": 0; "S[tud?] horses": 0; "Town Lots": 0.
Tennessee Records of Grainger County-Tax Lists, 1799, [TN State Library and Archives] FAMILY HISTORY LIBRARY film 464105
Selvage, Micel, Tennessee, Grainger County
Selvage, Micel, Male
List of taxable property "Capt Margraves Compt 1799"; Lands: 0; "W[hite?] Poles": 1; "B[lack?] Poles": 0; "S[tud?] horses": 0; "Town Lots": 0.
Tennessee Records of Grainger County-Tax Lists, 1799, [TN State Library and Archives] FAMILY HISTORY LIBRARY film 464105
Sevier, John, Territory South of Ohio River
Sevier, John, Male

On 14 Nov 1795 "William Charles Cole Claiborne of the County of Sullivan [was] appointed Brigade Major of the Brigade commanded by Brigadier General John Sevier."
Territorial Papers of the US - volume: 4 page: 470
Shelby, Isaac, Territory South of Ohio River, Sullivan County
Shelby, Isaac, Male
On 27 Jan 1796 he was designated Collector "of the County and public taxes for the year 1796" for Sullivan County.
Territorial Papers of the US - volume: 4 page: 471
Shelby, Isaac, Territory South of Ohio River, Sullivan County
Shelby, Isaac, Male
On 2 May 1795 he was appointed Sheriff for Sullivan County.
Territorial Papers of the US - volume: 4 page: 467
Shockley, Richard, Tennessee, Grainger County
Shockley, Richard, Male
"Tax List Capt Jenings District taken in by Wm Hancock. 1797"; "W[hites?]": ?; "B[lacks?]": 0; "L[and?]": ?; "S[tud?] H[orses?]": 0.
Tennessee Records of Grainger County-Tax Lists, 1797 [TN State Library and Archives] FAMILY HISTORY LIBRARY film 464105
Short, James, Tennessee, Grainger County
Short, James, Male
"List of Taxable Property Harris Company Taken by James Moore. 1798"; Land: 0; "W[hite?] Pole": 1; "B[lack?] Pole": 0; "S[tud?] Horse": 0.
Tennessee Records of Grainger County-Tax Lists, 1798, [TN State Library and Archives] FAMILY HISTORY LIBRARY film 464105
Sims, John, Territory South of Ohio River, Hawkins County
Sims, John, Male
On 1 Aug 1795 he was made a Captain in the militia for Hawkins County.
Territorial Papers of the US - volume: 4 page: 468
Sims, Littlepage, Territory South of Ohio River, Blount County
Sims, Littlepage, Male
On 27 Jan 1796 he was designated Collector "of the County and public taxes for the year 1796" for Blount County.
Territorial Papers of the US - volume: 4 page: 471
Sims, Littlepage, Territory South of Ohio River, Blount County

Sims, Littlepage,   Male
On 3 Aug 1795 he was made Sheriff for Blount County.
Territorial Papers of the US - volume: 4 page: 469
Singleton, John,   Territory South of Ohio River, Blount County
          Singleton, John,   Male
On 3 Aug 1795 he was made an Ensign for Blount County.
Territorial Papers of the US - volume: 4 page: 469
Smith, Aaron, Tennessee, Grainger County
          Smith, Aaron,   Male
"List of Taxable Property Harris Company Taken by James Moore. 1798"; Land: 400; "W[hite?] Pole": 0; "B[lack?] Pole": 1; "S[tud?] Horse": 0.
Tennessee Records of Grainger County-Tax Lists, 1798, [TN State Library and Archives]   FAMILY HISTORY LIBRARY film 464105
Smith, Georg, Tennessee, Grainger County
          Smith, Georg,   Male
"List of Taxable Property Harris Company Taken by James Moore. 1798"; Land: 200; "W[hite?] Pole": 2; "B[lack?] Pole": 0; "S[tud?] Horse": 0.
Tennessee Records of Grainger County-Tax Lists, 1798, [TN State Library and Archives]   FAMILY HISTORY LIBRARY film 464105
Smith, Josiah, Tennessee, Grainger County
          Smith, Josiah,   Male
"Tax List Capt Jenings District taken in by Wm Hancock. 1797"; "W[hites?]": 1; "B[lacks?]": 0; "L[and?]": 162; "S[tud?] H[orses?]": 0.
Tennessee Records of Grainger County-Tax Lists, 1797 [TN State Library and Archives]   FAMILY HISTORY LIBRARY film 464105
Smith, Thomas,   Tennessee,   Grainger County
          Smith, Thomas,   Male
"List of Taxable Property Harris Company Taken by James Moore. 1798"; Land: 250; "W[hite?] Pole": 1; "B[lack?] Pole": 0; "S[tud?] Horse": 0.
Tennessee Records of Grainger County-Tax Lists, 1798, [TN State Library and Archives]   FAMILY HISTORY LIBRARY film 464105
Snoddy, William,   Territory South of Ohio River, Sumner County
          Snoddy, William,   Male
On 17 Jan 1795 he was made a Captain in the Regiment of Infantry for Sumner County.
Territorial Papers of the US - volume: 4 page: 464
Spenjer, John, Tennessee, Grainger County

Spenjer, John,   Male
"Tax List Capt Jenings District taken in by Wm Hancock. 1797"; "W[hites?]": 1; "B[lacks?]": 2; "L[and?]": 300; "S[tud?] H[orses?]": 0.
Tennessee Records of Grainger County-Tax Lists, 1797 [TN State Library and Archives]   FAMILY HISTORY LIBRARY film 464105
Stinson, James,   Territory South of Ohio River, Washington District
          Stinson, James, Male
On 27 Nov 1795 he was "appointed Captain of Cavalry in the Regiment of Washington District."
Territorial Papers of the US - volume: 4 page: 470
Taylor, Parmenas,   Territory South of Ohio River, Hamilton District
          Taylor, Parmenas,   Male
On 7 Feb 1795 he was made Lieutenant Colonel Commandant in the Regiment of Cavalry for Hamilton District.
Territorial Papers of the US - volume: 4 page: 466
Tedford, George,   Territory South of Ohio River, Blount County
          Tedford, George,   Male
On 3 Aug 1795 he was made an Ensign for Blount County.
Territorial Papers of the US - volume: 4 page: 469
Tedford, Joseph,   Territory South of Ohio River, Blount County
          Tedford, Joseph,   Male
On 3 Aug 1795 he was made an Ensign for Blount County.
Territorial Papers of the US - volume: 4 page: 469
Temple, John, Territory South of Ohio River, Washington District
          Temple, John,   Male
On 27 Nov 1795 he was "appointed First Lieutenant of Cavalry in the Regiment of Washington District."
Territorial Papers of the US - volume: 4 page: 470
Thacker, Edward,   Tennessee,   Grainger County
          Thacker, Edward,   Male
"List of Taxable Property Harris Company Taken by James Moore. 1798"; Land: 0; "W[hite?] Pole": 1; "B[lack?] Pole": 0; "S[tud?] Horse": 0.
Tennessee Records of Grainger County-Tax Lists, 1798, [TN State Library and Archives]   FAMILY HISTORY LIBRARY film 464105
Thompson, James,   Tennessee,   Grainger County

Thompson, James,   Male
"List of Taxable Property Harris Company Taken by James Moore. 1798"; Land: 330; "W[hite?] Pole": 0; "B[lack?] Pole": 0; "S[tud?] Horse": 0.
Tennessee Records of Grainger County-Tax Lists, 1798, [TN State Library and Archives]   FAMILY HISTORY LIBRARY film 464105
Thompson, Jempel, Tennessee,   Grainger County
        Thompson, Jempel,   Male
"List of Taxable Property Harris Company Taken by James Moore. 1798"; Land: 0; "W[hite?] Pole": 1; "B[lack?] Pole": 0; "S[tud?] Horse": 0.
Tennessee Records of Grainger County-Tax Lists, 1798, [TN State Library and Archives]   FAMILY HISTORY LIBRARY film 464105
Thornberry, Richard, Tennessee,   Grainger County
        Thornberry, Richard,   Male
List of taxable property "Capt Margraves Compt 1799"; Lands: 150; "W[hite?] Poles": 1; "B[lack?] Poles": 0; "S[tud?] horses": 0; "Town Lots": 0.
Tennessee Records of Grainger County-Tax Lists, 1799, [TN State Library and Archives]   FAMILY HISTORY LIBRARY film 464105
Tremble, John,   Territory South of Ohio River, Blount County
        Tremble, John, Male
On 3 Aug 1795 he was made a Justice of the Peace for Blount County.
Territorial Papers of the US - volume: 4 page: 469
Trogdon, Ezekiel, Tennessee,   Grainger County
        Trogdon, Ezekiel,   Male
"List of Taxable Property Harris Company Taken by James Moore. 1798"; Land: 122; "W[hite?] Pole": 1; "B[lack?] Pole": 0; "S[tud?] Horse": 0.
Tennessee Records of Grainger County-Tax Lists, 1798, [TN State Library and Archives]   FAMILY HISTORY LIBRARY film 464105
Umphres, John, Tennessee,   Grainger County
        Umphres, John,   Male
"List of Taxable Property Harris Company Taken by James Moore. 1798"; Land: 0; "W[hite?] Pole": 1; "B[lack?] Pole": 0; "S[tud?] Horse": 0.
Tennessee Records of Grainger County-Tax Lists, 1798, [TN State Library and Archives]   FAMILY HISTORY LIBRARY film 464105

Underhill, Daniel, Tennessee,   Grainger County
        Underhill, Daniel,   Male
List of taxable property "Capt Margraves Compt 1799"; Lands: 50; "W[hite?] Poles": 1; "B[lack?] Poles": 0; "S[tud?] horses": 0; "Town Lots": 0.
Tennessee Records of Grainger County-Tax Lists, 1799, [TN State Library and Archives]   FAMILY HISTORY LIBRARY film 464105
Underhill, Wm, Tennessee,   Grainger County
        Underhill, Wm,   Male
"List of Taxable Property Harris Company Taken by James Moore. 1798"; Land: 0; "W[hite?] Pole": 1; "B[lack?] Pole": 0; "S[tud?] Horse": 0.
Tennessee Records of Grainger County-Tax Lists, 1798, [TN State Library and Archives]   FAMILY HISTORY LIBRARY film 464105
Vittetoe, Thomas, Tennessee,   Grainger County
        Vittetoe, Thomas,   Male
"List of Taxable Property Harris Company Taken by James Moore. 1798"; Land: 0; "W[hite?] Pole": 1; "B[lack?] Pole": 0; "S[tud?] Horse": 0.
Page 33 is out of order and can be found on the microfilm following page 202. Page 33 has no heading, but the columns appear to be the same as those on page 32 and so will be considered as a part of that series. The entries appear to be crossed out.
Tennessee Records of Grainger County-Tax Lists, 1798, [TN State Library and Archives]   FAMILY HISTORY LIBRARY film 464105
Walker, James,   Territory South of Ohio River, Jefferson County
        Walker, James, Male
On 8 Jul 1795 he was made a Lieutenant in the Regiment of Infantry for Jefferson County.
Territorial Papers of the US - volume: 4 page: 468
Wallace, Jesse,   Territory South of Ohio River, Hamilton District
        Wallace, Jesse, Male
On 28 Nov 1795 he was "appointed a Cornet in the Cavalry of the Regiment of the District of Hamilton."
Territorial Papers of the US - volume: 4 page: 470
Wallace, Joel, Territory South of Ohio River, Blount County
        Wallace, Joel,   Male

On 3 Aug 1795 he was made an Ensign for Blount County.
Territorial Papers of the US - volume: 4 page: 469
Wallace, Matthew, Territory South of Ohio River, Blount County
Wallace, Matthew, Male
On 3 Aug 1795 he was made a Justice of the Peace for Blount County.
Territorial Papers of the US - volume: 4 page: 469
Wallace, Matthew, Territory South of Ohio River, Blount County
Wallace, Matthew, Male
On 3 Aug 1795 he was made Second Lieutenant in the Cavalry for Blount County.
Territorial Papers of the US - volume: 4 page: 469
Wallace, William, Territory South of Ohio River, Blount County
Wallace, William, Male
On 3 Aug 1795 he was made a Justice of the Peace for Blount County.
Territorial Papers of the US - volume: 4 page: 469
Wallace, William, Territory South of Ohio River, Blount County
Wallace, William, Male
On 3 Aug 1795 he was made Register for Blount County.
Territorial Papers of the US - volume: 4 page: 469
Walters, Obediah, Tennessee, Grainger County
Walters, Obediah, Male
List of taxable property "Capt Margraves Compt 1799"; Lands: 200; "W[hite?] Poles": 1; "B[lack?] Poles": 0; "S[tud?] horses": 0; "Town Lots": 0.
Tennessee Records of Grainger County-Tax Lists, 1799, [TN State Library and Archives] FAMILY HISTORY LIBRARY film 464105
Walters, William, Tennessee, Grainger County
Walters, William, Male
"Tax List Capt Jenings District taken in by Wm Hancock. 1797"; "W[hites?]": 1; "B[lacks?]": 0; "L[and?]": 0; "S[tud?] H[orses?]": 0.
Tennessee Records of Grainger County-Tax Lists, 1797 [TN State Library and Archives] FAMILY HISTORY LIBRARY film 464105
Watson, Enis, Tennessee, Grainger County
Watson, Enis, Male
"List of Taxable Property Harris Company Taken by James Moore. 1798"; Land: 0; "W[hite?] Pole": 1; "B[lack?] Pole": 0; "S[tud?] Horse": 0.

Tennessee Records of Grainger County-Tax Lists, 1798, [TN State Library and Archives] FAMILY HISTORY LIBRARY film 464105
Watson, Thomas, Tennessee, Grainger County
Watson, Thomas, Male
"List of Taxable Property Harris Company Taken by James Moore. 1798"; Land: 0; "W[hite?] Pole": 1; "B[lack?] Pole": 0; "S[tud?] Horse": 0.
Tennessee Records of Grainger County-Tax Lists, 1798, [TN State Library and Archives] FAMILY HISTORY LIBRARY film 464105
Webster, William, Tennessee, Grainger County
Webster, William, Male
List of taxable property "Capt Margraves Compt 1799"; Lands: 0; "W[hite?] Poles": 1; "B[lack?] Poles": 0; "S[tud?] horses": 0; "Town Lots": 0.
Tennessee Records of Grainger County-Tax Lists, 1799, [TN State Library and Archives] FAMILY HISTORY LIBRARY film 464105
Westmoreland, David, Tennessee, Grainger County
Westmoreland, David, Male
"List of Taxable Property Harris Company Taken by James Moore. 1798"; Land: 0; "W[hite?] Pole": 1; "B[lack?] Pole": 0; "S[tud?] Horse": 0.
Tennessee Records of Grainger County-Tax Lists, 1798, [TN State Library and Archives] FAMILY HISTORY LIBRARY film 464105
Westmoreland, John, Tennessee, Grainger County
Westmoreland, John, Male
"List of Taxable Property Harris Company Taken by James Moore. 1798"; Land: 0; "W[hite?] Pole": 1; "B[lack?] Pole": 0; "S[tud?] Horse": 0.
Tennessee Records of Grainger County-Tax Lists, 1798, [TN State Library and Archives] FAMILY HISTORY LIBRARY film 464105
White, James, Territory South of Ohio River, Davidson or Sumner Counties
White, James, Male
He resigned, ca 25 Apr 1795, as a member of the General Assembly.
Territorial Papers of the US - volume: 4 page: 467
White, James, Col: Territory South of Ohio River, Knox County
White, James, Col: Male
List, 21 Dec 1795, of members of Knoxville Convention.

Territorial Papers of the US - volume: 4 page: 415
White, Nathin, Tennessee, Grainger County
White, Nathin, Male
"List of Taxable Property Harris Company Taken by James Moore. 1798"; Land: 0; "W[hite?] Pole": 1; "B[lack?] Pole": 0; "S[tud?] Horse": 0.
Tennessee Records of Grainger County-Tax Lists, 1798, [TN State Library and Archives] FAMILY HISTORY LIBRARY film 464105
Whitehead, Robert, Tennessee, Grainger County
Whitehead, Robert, Male
"List of Taxable Property Harris Company Taken by James Moore. 1798"; Land: 0; "W[hite?] Pole": ?; "B[lack?] Pole": 0; "S[tud?] Horse": 0.
Tennessee Records of Grainger County-Tax Lists, 1798, [TN State Library and Archives] FAMILY HISTORY LIBRARY film 464105
Whitlock, James, Tennessee, Grainger County
Whitlock, James, Male
"List of Taxable Property Harris Company Taken by James Moore. 1798"; Land: 400; "W[hite?] Pole": 1; "B[lack?] Pole": 0; "S[tud?] Horse": 0.
Tennessee Records of Grainger County-Tax Lists, 1798, [TN State Library and Archives] FAMILY HISTORY LIBRARY film 464105
Williams, John, Territory South of Ohio River, Sumner County
Williams, John, Male
On 17 Jan 1795 he was made a Lieutenant in the Regiment of Infantry for Sumner County.
Territorial Papers of the US - volume: 4 page: 464
Williams, John, Territory South of Ohio River, Jefferson County
Williams, John, Male
On 8 Jul 1795 he was made an Ensign in the Regiment of Infantry for Jefferson County.
Territorial Papers of the US - volume: 4 page: 468
Williams, John, Tennessee, Grainger County
Williams, John, Male
"List of Taxable Property Harris Company Taken by James Moore. 1798"; Land: 200; "W[hite?] Pole": 0; "B[lack?] Pole": 0; "S[tud?] Horse": 0.
Tennessee Records of Grainger County-Tax Lists, 1798, [TN State Library and Archives] FAMILY HISTORY LIBRARY film 464105

Williams, Jonathan, Tennessee, Grainger County
Williams, Jonathan, Male
"List of Taxable Property Harris Company Taken by James Moore. 1798"; Land: 0; "W[hite?] Pole": 1; "B[lack?] Pole": 0; "S[tud?] Horse": 0.
Tennessee Records of Grainger County-Tax Lists, 1798, [TN State Library and Archives] FAMILY HISTORY LIBRARY film 464105
Williams, Oliver, Territory South of Ohio River, Davidson County
Williams, Oliver, Male
On 14 Jul 1795 he was appointed Deputy Sheriff for Davidson County.
Territorial Papers of the US - volume: 4 page: 468
Wilson, David, Territory South of Ohio River, Davidson or Sumner Counties
Wilson, David, Male
He resigned, ca 25 Apr 1795, as a member of the General Assembly.
Territorial Papers of the US - volume: 4 page: 467
Wilson, James, Territory South of Ohio River, Jefferson County
Wilson, James, Male
On 6 Feb 1795 he was made a Justice of the Peace for Jefferson County.
Territorial Papers of the US - volume: 4 page: 465
Wilson, John, Territory South of Ohio River, Jefferson County
Wilson, John, Male
On 2 May 1795 he was appointed Deputy Sheriff for Jefferson County.
Territorial Papers of the US - volume: 4 page: 467
Wilson, William, Territory South of Ohio River, Greene County
Wilson, William, Male
On 11 Jul 1795 he was made a Justice of the Peace for Greene County.
Territorial Papers of the US - volume: 4 page: 468
Wilson, Wm, Tennessee, Grainger County
Wilson, Wm, Male
"List of Taxable Property Harris Company Taken by James Moore. 1798"; Land: 0; "W[hite?] Pole": 1; "B[lack?] Pole": 0; "S[tud?] Horse": 0.
Tennessee Records of Grainger County-Tax Lists, 1798, [TN State Library and Archives] FAMILY HISTORY LIBRARY film 464105
Wines, Enoch, Tennessee, Grainger County
Wines, Enoch, Male

"List of Taxable Property Harris Company Taken by James Moore. 1798"; Land: 0; "W[hite?] Pole": 1; "B[lack?] Pole": 0; "S[tud?] Horse": 0.
Tennessee Records of Grainger County-Tax Lists, 1798, [TN State Library and Archives]   FAMILY HISTORY LIBRARY film 464105
Wydner, Henry,   Tennessee,   Grainger County
         Wydner, Henry,   Male
List of taxable property "Capt Margraves Compt 1799"; Lands: 0; "W[hite?] Poles": 1; "B[lack?] Poles": 0; "S[tud?] horses": "1 horse[?] Stan $2."; "Town Lots": 0.
Tennessee Records of Grainger County-Tax Lists, 1799, [TN State Library and Archives]   FAMILY HISTORY LIBRARY film 464105
Wydner, Lewis,   Tennessee,   Grainger County
         Wydner, Lewis,   Male
List of taxable property "Capt Margraves Compt 1799"; Lands: 450; "W[hite?] Poles": 0; "B[lack?] Poles": 3; "S[tud?] horses": 0; "Town Lots": 0.

Tennessee Records of Grainger County-Tax Lists, 1799, [TN State Library and Archives]   FAMILY HISTORY LIBRARY film 464105
Wyrick, William,   Tennessee,   Grainger County
         Wyrick, William,   Male
List of taxable property "Capt Margraves Compt 1799"; Lands: 0; "W[hite?] Poles": 1; "B[lack?] Poles": 0; "S[tud?] horses": 0; "Town Lots": 0.
Tennessee Records of Grainger County-Tax Lists, 1799, [TN State Library and Archives]   FAMILY HISTORY LIBRARY film 464105
Yancey, A,   Tennessee, Grainger County
         Yancey, A,   Male
         His name is at the end of the list after the text: "Recorded at Length".
"Tax List Capt Jenings District taken in by Wm Hancock. 1797"; "W[hites?]": 0; "B[lacks?]": 0; "L[and?]": 0; "S[tud?] H[orses?]": 0.
Tennessee Records of Grainger County-Tax Lists, 1797 [TN State Library and Archives]   FAMILY HISTORY LIBRARY film 464105

STEMMONS PUBLISHING, 1078 Shields Lane, South Jordan, Utah 84095, 801-254-2152 (Call between 9:00 a.m. and 5:00 p.m. Monday through Friday. If no one answers, please leave a message.), stemmonspublishing@gmail.com

The importance of census records and other population lists cannot be overstated in terms of the help they are in locating people in a specific area. This allows one to examine other records in that area. This is one of our main goals and why we do business. What we are trying to accomplish is a work in progress. We hope to improve as we go along. Thank you for your patience.

Petitions are an important example of these population lists.

Thank you for the opportunity to serve you.

Sincerely,
John Stemmons

A COMPLETE LIST OF OUR GENEALOGY BOOKS

AL-01 **ALABAMA 1800 PETITIONERS [-1804]**© Compiled by John D Stemmons, 2021. This book compiled from *Territorial Papers of the United States* contains 253 entries for a very early period in Alabama's history. It may contain some biographical details and clues to prior residence. It can help substitute for the missing federal census. For information on how to obtain this book search by the title or "Books by John Stemmons" at Amazon.com. This comes automatically with a paperback binding. It includes but is not limited to petitions regarding:

- Seeking new territory due to the rapid migration from Georgia, etc.
- Petition seeking confirmation of land grants obtained from other governments.

36 Pages $7.20

AL-02 **ALABAMA 1810 PETITIONERS, ETC., [1805-1814]**© Compiled by John D Stemmons, 2021. This book compiled from *Territorial Papers of the United States* contains 1687 entries for a very early period in Alabama's history. It includes a census of

Madison County, taken Jan 1809. It may contain some biographical details and clues to prior residence. It can help substitute for the missing federal census. For information on how to obtain this book search by the title or "Books by John Stemmons" at Amazon.com. This comes automatically with a paperback binding. It includes but is not limited to petitions regarding:

- Issues relating to land.
- Petition of inhabitants east of Pearl River seeking to form a new territory.
- 1809 census of Madison County.
- Inhabitants of Tombigbee seeking for their purchases from the Spanish to be duty free at "Fort Stoddart".

176 Pages $35.20

AL-03 ALABAMA 1820 PETITIONERS, ETC., [1815-1824]©
Compiled by John D Stemmons, 2021. This book compiled from *Territorial Papers of the United States* contains 3913 entries for a fast-growing period in Alabama's history. It may contain some biographical details and clues to prior residence. It can help substitute for the missing federal census. For information on how to obtain this book search by the title or "Books by John Stemmons" at Amazon.com. This comes automatically with a paperback binding. It includes but is not limited to petitions regarding:

- Merchants and traders of St. Stephens seeking to establish that town as a port of delivery.
- Inhabitants of eastern part of MS territory, who lost much income/property in the wars with England & Indians.
- Inhabitants of Alabama Territory opposing the "settlements on the western side of the Mobile & Tombigby rivers" being made part of Mississippi.
- List of Letters, 9 Jan 1819, remaining in Huntsville Post Office.
- Issues about military and local officers.
- Memorial, ref. 20 Jan 1817, to Congress from inhabitants of Mobile complaining that Ft Charlotte is indefensible.

407 Pages $81.40

AR-01 ARKANSAS PETITIONERS, ETC. 1800, 1810 [1795-1814]© Compiled by John D Stemmons, 2021. This book compiled from *Territorial Papers of the United States* contains 261 entries and is a partial replacement for the missing federal censuses of 1800 and 1810. As a result, it is a very helpful resource in establishing residence of people in Arkansas during that early formative period in the state's history. These people include some of earliest you will find that established the foundation of what was to become the great state that Arkansas now is. This also makes it possible to determine what other records might be available for further research. Some additional biographical details may be included, and possible relationships with others may be revealed. For information on how to obtain this book search by the title or "Books by John Stemmons" at Amazon.com. This comes automatically with a paperback binding. It includes but is not limited to petitions regarding:

- Issues relating to land.
- Inhabitants of Arkansas District expressing concern about the hostile attitude of the Cherokees nearby.
- Issues about military and local officers.

43 Pages $8.60

AR-02 ARKANSAS PETITIONERS, ETC. 1820 [1815-1824]©
Compiled by John D Stemmons, 2021. This book compiled from *Territorial Papers of the United States* contains 1936 entries and is a partial replacement for the missing federal census of 1820. As a result, it is a very helpful resource in establishing residence of people in Arkansas during that fast-growing territorial period prior to becoming a state. Unfortunately, the 1820 census is not available to help track these people. That is why this new book can help. It is even better in some respects than the census because it helps us understand some of the challenges they faced. It also makes possible the determination of

other records that might be available for further research. Some additional biographical details may be included, and possible relationships with others may be revealed. Even the names of some Native Americans are included as well as a few potential residents of Oklahoma. For information on how to obtain this book search by the title or "Books by John Stemmons" at Amazon.com. This comes automatically with a paperback binding. It includes but is not limited to petitions regarding:

- Issues relating to land.
- Issues relating to Native Americans.
- Citizens of Arkansas County describing the good location of the Town of Arkansas.
- Appointments about military and local officers, etc.
- Inhabitants of Arkansas and Phillips Counties seeking a mail route from the Town of Arkansas to the "Post of Ouachita in Louisianna."
- Abstract of Grand and Petit Jurors, Oct term, 1824 listing compensation for their attendance at a Superior Court held at Little Rock.

216 Pages $43.20

1001-GEORGIA PETITIONS 1778-1784© Compiled by John D Stemmons, 2004. This book contains 256 entries for a very early period in Georgia's history. For information on how to obtain this book search by the title or "Books by John Stemmons" at Amazon.com. This comes automatically with a paperback binding. It includes but is not limited to petitions regarding:

- A desire for a new district.
- A request for local courts.
- Issues about military and local officers.
- Request for protection against enemies.
- A request for pardon, amnesty, etc.
- Description of hardship.

44 pages $8.80

1002-GEORGIA PETITIONS 1785-1794© Compiled by John D Stemmons, 2004. Contains 3720 entries which includes about 25% of the heads of household in Georgia at that time. As such this publication is an excellent substitute for the missing Georgia 1790 federal census. It even includes many names for Burke and Washington Counties which suffered severe record loss in the early years. For information on how to obtain this book search by the title or "Books by John Stemmons" at Amazon.com. This comes automatically with a paperback binding. It includes but is not limited to petitions regarding:

- Issues regarding local agencies, boundary changes, etc.
- Issues regarding religion and churches.
- Issues about military and local officers.
- Asking for measures to control slaves.
- Recommendation for a business opportunity.
- Seeking resolution of land problems, land fraud, etc.
- Asking for increased tobacco inspection fees.
- Request for protection against Indians.
- Issues about crimes, pardon, amnesty, etc.
- Description of hardship.

367 pages $73.40

IL-01 ILLINOIS PETITIONS, ETC., 1760-1810 [1755-1814]©
Compiled by John D Stemmons, 2021, this book contains 3680 names from *The Territorial Papers of the U.S.* This covers a period of time even before the federal census of 1790. And while no federal censuses exists for Illinois from 1790-1810, these records nicely substitute for those missing documents. It should be noted that 1004-**A PARTIAL CENSUS FOR INDIANA TERRITORY 1810** includes most if not all the names for 1810. A study to determine that they were the same was inconclusive and so, just in the outside chance there might be some that were not the same, it was felt that they should be included. The convenience of having them together outweighs their exclusion.

These records include an incredible amount of information about these early people. One can see the change from a mostly French culture to that of English. The transition was not always peaceful. Included are census records, lists of inhabitants, and much more. While the federal censuses are missing that would help track these people, these records are even better in some respects than the census because it helps us understand some of the challenges they faced. That is why this new book can help. Some additional biographical details may be included, plus possible relationships with other family members. For information on how to obtain this book search by the title or "Books by John Stemmons" at Amazon.com. This comes automatically with a paperback binding. It includes but is not limited to petitions regarding:

- Issues relating to land.
- Issues relating to Native Americans.
- List of inhabitants at Kaskaskias before 1783.
- Appointments about military and local officers, etc.
- Lands claimed and possessed by inhabitants of the District of Cahokia on or before 1783 that still existed after 29 May 1790.
- Applications for lands in the District of Cahokia by persons claiming as settlers under the state of Virginia, if the settlements were made on or before 1783 that still existed after 29 May 1790.
- List of families at the Prairie du Pont, undated, but enclosed in St. Clair's report 10 Feb 1791.

349 Pages $69.80

IN-01 THE TERRITORY NORTHWEST OF THE RIVER OHIO, PETITIONERS, ETC., 1790-1800 [1785-1804] (Present day Indiana)© Compiled by John D Stemmons, 2021. This book was compiled from *Territorial Papers of the United States.* 1790 contains 242 names found on petitions, etc., including a census of heads of household for Vincennes. 1800 only includes 76 names and so is not as valuable as 1790. The population of Indiana would have increased significantly between 1790 and 1800. This is still a very early time prior to Indiana becoming a state. Unfortunately, there is no 1790 or 1800 census existing to help track these people. Therefore, we must do what we can with what is available. That is why this new book is so helpful. It is even better in some respects than the census because it helps us understand some of the challenges they faced. It also makes possible the determination of other records that might be available for further research such as land grants. Even the names of some Native Americans are listed. Some additional biographical details may be included, plus possible relationships with other family members. For information on how to obtain this book search by the title or "Books by John Stemmons" at Amazon.com. This comes automatically with a paperback binding. It includes but is not limited to petitions regarding:

- Issues relating to land.
- Heads of families settled at Post Vincennes on or before 1783 and residents at this time [13 Jul 1790] who are entitled to donation lands.
- Issues relating to Native Americans.
- Inhabitants of Vincennes who migrated to Vincennes around 1786 and received land, but never obtained a deed.
- Appointments about military and local officers, etc.

38 Pages $7.60

1003-INDIANA ELECTION RETURNS 1809, 1812© Compiled by John D and E. Diane Stemmons, 2004. This compilation of 3576 entries includes the names found in the territorial election returns which documents are in the Indiana Historical Society. Also included is a poll book of an election for Dearborn County in 1809 as found in *Territorial Papers of the United States.* All entries in this book are also found in *A Partial Census for Indiana Territory 1810.* The book *Indiana Election Returns, 1809, 1812* was compiled for just the election returns simply because they are one entire record source and may have some value in that. For information on how to obtain this

book search by the title or "Books by John Stemmons" at Amazon.com. This comes automatically with a paperback binding.
285 pages $57.00

1004-A PARTIAL CENSUS FOR INDIANA TERRITORY 1810© Compiled by John D and E. Diane Stemmons, 2021. With 8602 entries this book includes name lists found in *Territorial Papers of the United States* for Indiana Territory during the period 1805 through 1814. It also provides the names in *Indiana Election Returns 1809, 1812* listed above. Since there were approximately 4300 heads of households in the territory in 1810, *A Partial Census for Indiana Territory 1810* probably lists virtually every head of household in Indiana Territory for the time period. It makes an excellent substitute for the missing federal census for 1810. In addition, it includes names of people living in what is now Illinois, but which was part of Indiana Territory before 1809. Therefore, *A Partial Census for Indiana Territory 1810* is also a partial census of Illinois in the years between 1805 to 1809. For information on how to obtain this book search by the title or "Books by John Stemmons" at Amazon.com. This comes automatically with a paperback binding. It includes but is not limited to petitions regarding:

- Issues relating to land.
- Heads of families settled at Post Vincennes on or before 1783 and residents at this time [13 Jul 1790] who are entitled to donation lands.
- Issues relating to Native Americans.
- Inhabitants of Vincennes who migrated to Vincennes around 1786 and received land, but never obtained a deed.
- Appointments about military and local officers, etc.

574 pages $114.80

KY-01 KENTUCKY 1800, BARREN COUNTY TAX BOOK© Compiled by John D Stemmons, 2021. It contains 494 names from the Barren County tax list and 1 from *The Territorial Papers of the U.S.* Even though the 1800 census is missing this list it provides an amazing amount of information that substitutes nicely for that missing census, including white and black males aged 16-21 and those 21 and over. This is the kind of information one would expect to find on the census for that period. This list includes all taxable heads of household. Some additional biographical details may be included, plus possible relationships with other family members. The names of the blacks may be found in court, land, and probate records. For information on how to obtain this book search by the title or "Books by John Stemmons" at Amazon.com. This comes automatically with a paperback binding.
65 Pages $13.00

LA-01 ARKANSAS PETITIONS 1800 [1795-1804] and ORLEANS TERRITORY (NOW LOUISIANA) PETITIONS, ETC., 1800 [1795-1804]© Compiled by John D Stemmons, 2021. This book was compiled from *Territorial Papers of the United States* and contains 495 names for Louisiana and 3 from Arkansas. Since no federal census exists for Arkansas and Louisiana for 1800, these records nicely substitute for those missing documents. These records include an incredible amount of information about these early people. While the federal censuses are missing that would help track these people, these records are even better in some respects than the census because it helps us understand some of the challenges they faced. That is why this new book can help. Some additional biographical details may be included, plus possible relationships with other family members. For information on how to obtain this book search by the title or "Books by John Stemmons" at Amazon.com. This comes automatically with a paperback binding. It includes but is not limited to petitions regarding:

- Inhabitants of Pointe Coupee to Gov. Claiborne, requesting military aid because of fears of a slave revolt.
- Characterization of New Orleans residents, 1 July 1804.

- Address from the free people of color Jan. 1804, volunteering for military service.
- Memorial to Congress from merchants of New Orleans, 9 Jan 1804, offering allegiance to the US.
- Appointments about military and local officers, etc.

47 Pages $9.40

MO-01 MISSOURI PETITIONERS, ETC., 1780-1820 [1775-1824]© Compiled by John D Stemmons, 2021. This book was compiled from *Territorial Papers of the United States* and contains 1 name for 1780, 12 names for 1790, 19 names for 1800, 5057 names for 1810, and 1509 names for 1820. The later lists begin to approach the number needed to include most heads of household, and nicely substitute for missing or no censuses. These records include an incredible amount of information about these early people. While censuses help track people, the records this book includes are even better in some respects than the census because it helps us understand some of their personal feelings and challenges, they faced. Some additional biographical details may be included, plus possible relationships with other family members. For information on how to obtain this book search by the title or "Books by John Stemmons" at Amazon.com. This comes automatically with a paperback binding. It includes but is not limited to petitions, etc., regarding:
- Resolution recommending distinction between Americans and Frenchmen should be done away.
- Letter from U.S. President to Chief White Hairs and the warriors of the Osages, informing them of the Lewis and Clark expedition, and promising them a resident agent.
- Many petitions, etc., expressing their support and confidence in Governor Wilkinson. He was involved in scandals and controversies.
- Memorial recommending replacements for Governor Wilkinson.
- Petition expressing concern about changing the form of territorial government before they are adequately prepared.
- Memorial concerning the large number of their Spanish land claims that are being rejected.
- Lists of civil and military officers.
- Petition seeking a grant of a township of land for the support of the school as had been done in other areas.
- Petition seeking pre-emption rights for the services given in defending the frontier in Boon's Lick Settlement around 1815.
- Petitions relating to the New Madrid & Little Prairie earthquake.
- Petitions asking for new post offices and routes, etc.

552 pages $110.40

MI-01 MICHIGAN PETITIONS, ETC. 1790-1810 [1785-1814]© Compiled by John D Stemmons, 2021. This book was compiled from *Territorial Papers of the United States*. It contains 1 name for 1790, 794 names for 1800, and 1335 names for 1810. Clearly, that is not enough for 1790, but the others begin to approach the number needed. Especially is this so for 1810 because we are fortunate enough to have much of what appears to be the federal 1810 census. Since no federal census exists for 1800, the records nicely substitute for those missing documents. These records include an incredible amount of information about these early people. While censuses help track people, the records this book includes are even better in some respects than the census because it helps us understand some of their personal feelings and challenges, they faced. Some additional biographical details may be included, plus possible relationships with other family members. For information on how to obtain this book search by the title or "Books by John Stemmons" at Amazon.com. This comes automatically with a paperback binding. It includes but is not limited to petitions regarding:
- Inhabitants of Detroit seeking new territory because of distance to travel to the headquarters of Indiana Territory.
- Appointments about military and local officers, etc.
- Inhabitants of Wayne County seeking clarification of the status of their land.
- 1810 Census of the District of Detroit.
- Inhabitants of Michigan Ter. seeking time to file claims to their land.
- List, 23 Jul 1812, of patents received from the General Land Office for private claims in the District of Detroit.
- Petition from inhabitants of Michigan Territory asking that the new territorial code be printed also in French.
- Petition to Thomas Jefferson, from inhabitants of Michigan Territory complaining of Governor William Hull and Supreme Court Chief Justice Augustus B. Woodward.

222 Pages $44.40

MS-01 MISSISSIPPI TERRITORIAL PETITIONERS, ETC. 1800 [1795-1804]© Compiled by John D Stemmons, 2021. This book was compiled from *Territorial Papers of the United States and* contains 2566 names found on petitions, etc., from Mississippi Territory for this time period. This was during a fast-growing era prior to Mississippi becoming a state. Unfortunately, there is no 1800 census existing to help track these people. That is why this new book can help. It is even better in some respects than the census because it helps us understand some of the challenges they faced. It also makes possible the determination of other records that might be available for further research such as Spanish land grants. Some additional biographical details may be included, plus possible relationships with other family members. For information on how to obtain this book search by the title or "Books by John Stemmons" at Amazon.com. This comes automatically with a paperback binding. It includes but is not limited to petitions regarding:
- Citizens of territory asking land office to be in the area, settlers have pre-emption right, & suffrage be for males of age and US citizens & residents of territory for 6 months.
- Memorial by citizens of the territory, who obtained land before the area became part of the US.
- Testimonials, ca 1802, by individuals regarding the service of John Steele, secretary of the territory.
- Memorial by citizens of the territory seeking that "moderate grants [be] made to actual settlers on unappropriated lands,"
- Merchants of Natchez, complaining of the extra duties they must pay for merchandise shipped from the US.

209 Pages $41.80

MS-02 MISSISSIPPI TERRITORIAL PETITIONS, ETC. 1810 [1805-1814] and WEST FLORIDA 1820 PETITIONERS [1815-1824]© Compiled by John D Stemmons, 2021. This book was compiled from *Territorial Papers of the United States* and contains 1061 names found on petitions, etc., from Mississippi Territory for the period 1810 [1805-1814]. It also includes a list of 76 names on a petition to Congress, 11 Dec 1816, by inhabitants of Jackson County, Mississippi Territory, many of whom settled on land in West Florida while under Spanish control and now seek for their grant to be confirmed by the US. It is being included with Mississippi Territory because it is basically the same time period and place of residence. This was during a fast-growing time prior to Mississippi and Florida becoming states. Unfortunately, there is no 1810 or 1820 census existing to help track these people. That is why this new book can help. It is even better in some respects than the census because it helps us understand some of the challenges they faced. It also makes possible the determination of other records that might be available for further research. Some additional biographical details may be included, and possible relationships with others may be revealed. For information on how to obtain this book search by the title or "Books by John Stemmons" at Amazon.com. This comes automatically with a paperback binding. It includes but is not limited to petitions regarding:

- Inhabitants of the territory seeking adjustment of land claims obtained from the British Government.
- Inhabitants of the territory seek for a road to be built that follows the Pearl River which would shorten the route from Nashville to New Orleans.
- Inhabitants of Amite and Wilkinson Counties seek establishment of a post office.
- Memorial by citizens of the territory (Americans by birth?) seeking a postponement of statehood for the territory.
- Inhabitants of Jackson Co., Mississippi Territory, many of whom settled on land in West Florida while under Spanish control seek for their grant to be confirmed by the US.

108 Pages $21.60

NJ-01-NEW JERSEY PETITIONS 1740, 1745 THROUGH 1754©
Compiled by John D Stemmons, 2021. It contains 740 entries for a period of time in New Jersey when records are sparse. While that may not seem like very many names, it was during the time when the population was small, and the residence of people was sometimes hard to track. In looking through these petitions, it appears that the people of this era had basically the same concerns as we have. One can see the forces of democracy beginning to stir that were to result in independence from Great Britain just a short three decades away. We can obtain a hint of the personal concerns of these people and what was important to them in this exciting historical time. Even at this time of great distress and hardship life had to go on. These petitions are almost like an open window into the lives of these people. For information on how to obtain this book search by the title or "Books by John Stemmons" at Amazon.com. This comes automatically with a paperback binding. It includes but is not limited to petitions regarding:
- Issues regarding exports and imports.
- Issues regarding devaluation of currency, money supply, etc.
- Issues regarding local agencies, boundary changes, etc.
- Seeking new legislation.
- Issues about military and government officers.
- Seeking resolution of land problems, etc.
- Protesting against the great number of taverns.
- Resolution of tax issues.
- Issues about crimes, pardon, amnesty, etc.

84 pages $16.80

NJ-02-NEW JERSEY PETITIONS 1755-1764© Compiled by John D Stemmons, 2004. Contains 2389 entries from many petitions submitted because of concerns about the French and Indian War. This book is an excellent census substitute. For information on how to obtain this book search by the title or "Books by John Stemmons" at Amazon.com. This comes automatically with a paperback binding. It includes petitions regarding:
- Issues regarding local agencies, boundary changes, etc.
- Issues about roads, bridges, etc.
- Opposition to importing slaves.
- Seeking naturalization.
- Seeking new legislation.
- Issues about military and government affairs.
- Request for reimbursement from the government.
- Request for protection against enemies.
- Seeking resolution of land problems, etc.
- Protesting against dispensing of "spirituous liquors"
- Issues about crimes, pardon, amnesty, etc.
- Description of hardship.

246 pages $49.20

NJ-03-NEW JERSEY PETITIONS 1765-1774© Compiled by John D Stemmons, 2004. This book contains 806 entries. While a small percent of the population, it represents the time leading up to the Revolution. For information on how to obtain this book search by the title or "Books by John Stemmons" at Amazon.com. This comes automatically with a paperback binding. It includes but is not limited to petitions regarding:
- Issues regarding agriculture, exports and imports.
- Request for permission to beg, financial support, etc.
- Issues about religion and churches.
- Request for medical standards.
- Issues regarding devaluation of currency, money supply, etc.
- Issues regarding local agencies, boundary changes, etc.
- Issues on hunting, fishing, etc.
- Issues about roads, bridges, etc.
- Issues relating to slavery.
- Issues about military and government affairs.
- Seeking resolution of land problems, etc.
- Issues about crimes, pardon, amnesty, etc.

99 pages $19.80

NJ-04-NEW JERSEY PETITIONS 1775-1784© Compiled by John D Stemmons, 2005. This book contains 6201 entries which is about 29% of the heads of household living in New Jersey at that time (not counting duplicate names.) It represents the historic period during the Revolution. For information on how to obtain this book search by the title or "Books by John Stemmons" at Amazon.com. This comes automatically with a paperback binding. It includes but is not limited to petitions regarding:
- Issues regarding trade, exports, and imports.
- Issues regarding devaluation of currency, money supply, price controls, etc.
- Issues on religion and churches.
- Issues regarding local agencies, boundary changes or disputes, etc.
- Issues on court cases.
- Request for guardianship of children.
- Issues about roads, bridges, canals, etc.
- Issues on slavery.
- Seeking new legislation or repealing old laws.
- Issues about military and government affairs and officers.
- Issues about payment from the government.
- Issues on independence and the Revolutionary War.
- Request for protection against enemies.
- Seeking resolution of property and land problems, etc.
- Issues about crimes, pardon, amnesty, etc.
- Resolution of tax issues.

559 pages $111.80

NJ-05-NEW JERSEY PETITIONS 1785-1794 Volumes 1-2©
Compiled by John D Stemmons, 2005. This book contains 10,353 entries which covers about 35% of the heads of household for that time, not counting duplicate names. For information on how to obtain this book search by the title or "Books by John Stemmons" at Amazon.com. This comes automatically with a paperback binding. It includes but is not limited to petitions regarding:
- Economic issues regarding the devaluation of currency, public debt, etc.
- Issues on religion and churches.
- Issues regarding counties and towns, etc.
- Issues on court cases.
- Issues regarding hunting on private property, fishing, etc.
- Issues about roads, bridges, canals, ferries, etc.
- Issues relating to schools.
- Issues on slavery.
- Seeking new legislation or repealing existing laws.
- Issues about military and government affairs and officers.
- Seeking payment from the government.

- Expressing approval of the U.S. Constitution.
- Seeking resolution of property and land problems, etc.
- Issues about crimes, pardon, amnesty, etc.
- Resolution of tax issues.

Volume 1, A Through K, pages 462	$92.40
Volume 2, L Through Z, pages 470	$94.00

NJ-06 NEW JERSEY PETITIONERS, ETC., 1800 [1795-1804] Volumes 1-3© Compiled by John Stemmons, 2021. All volumes of this book contain 13,144 names. Unlike the tax ratables, these records cover the entire state for the period just after the Revolutionary War These records provide a place of residence which can lead to other records to search. For information on how to obtain this book search by the title or "Books by John Stemmons" at Amazon.com. This comes automatically with a paperback binding. It includes but is not limited to petitions regarding:

- Public buildings including poor house, taverns, banks, etc.
- Issues on religion and churches.
- Issues regarding counties and towns, etc.
- Issues on court cases.
- Concerning voting opportunities
- Issues about roads, bridges, canals, ferries, water rights, storage of gunpowder, etc.
- Issues relating to schools.
- Issues on slavery.
- Seeking new legislation or repealing existing laws.
- Issues about military and government affairs and officers.
- Seeking payment from the government.
- Seeking resolution of property and land problems, etc.
- Issues about crimes, pardon, amnesty, etc.
- Resolution of tax issues.

Volume 1, A Through E, pages 423	$84.60
Volume 2, F Through R, pages 529	$105.80
Volume 3, S Through Z, pages 358	$71.60

NJ-07 NEW JERSEY TAX RATABLES, 1770 [1765-1774] This book contains 2373 names of those who are taxable. They do include important details about the property they held and may provide clues regarding relationship, etc. For information on how to obtain this book search by the title or "Books by John Stemmons" at Amazon.com. This comes automatically with a paperback binding.

250 pages	$50.00

NJ-08 NEW JERSEY TAX RATABLES, 1780 [1775-1784] This book contains 4358 names of those who are taxable. It includes important details about the property they held and may provide clues regarding relationship, etc. For information on how to obtain this book search by the title or "Books by John Stemmons" at Amazon.com. This comes automatically with a paperback binding.

440 pages	$88.00

NJ-09 NEW JERSEY TAX RATABLES, 1790 [1785-1794] This book contains 2307 names of those who are taxable. Unfortunately, Burlington and Cape May counties are not covered by this period. We are fortunate though in have the petitions that cover the same time. It is interesting to compare the two sets of records. They were not combined because that would make the books too large. The tax ratables do include important details about the property they held and may provide clues regarding relationship, etc. For information on how to obtain this book search by the title or "Books by John Stemmons" at Amazon.com. This comes automatically with a paperback binding.

268 pages	$53.60

NJ-10 NEW JERSEY TAX RATABLES, 1800 [1795-1804] , Volumes 1-2 This book contains 8396 names of those who are taxable. It includes important details about the property they held and may provide clues regarding relationship, etc. For information on how

to obtain this book search by the title or "Books by John Stemmons" at Amazon.com. This comes automatically with a paperback binding.

Volume 1, A Through K, pages 456	$91.20
Volume 2, L Through Z, pages 449	$89.80

NC-01 NORTH CAROLINA PETITIONERS, ETC. 1780 [1775-1784]© Compiled by John Stemmons, 2021. This book contains 4866 names and was assembled from records located at the North Carolina State Archives. This was before the federal census was taken and is a valuable resource for locating people in this early time. Included are some names from what is now, Tennessee. For information on how to obtain this book search by the title or "Books by John Stemmons" at Amazon.com. This comes automatically with a paperback binding.

- Economic issues regarding the devaluation of currency, public debt, etc.
- Issues on religion and churches.
- Issues regarding counties and towns, etc.
- Issues regarding hunting on private property, fishing, etc.
- Issues about roads, bridges, canals, ferries, etc.
- Seeking new legislation or repealing existing laws.
- Issues about military and government affairs and officers.
- Seeking resolution of property and land problems, etc.
- Issues about crimes, pardon, amnesty, etc.

568 pages	$113.60

1009-ROWAN COUNTY, NORTH CAROLINA TAX LISTS 1758/1759, 1761, 1768, 1778, 1779© Compiled by John D and E. Diane Stemmons, 2004. This publication serves as a census for Rowan County for about three decades which includes two major conflicts, the French and Indian and Revolutionary wars. Thus, one may be able to track individuals that stayed in the county over a significant period of time. Sometimes sons and slaves are given plus other important information. These tax lists are listed alphabetically in three separate sections.

218 pages	$43.60

OH-01 TERRITORY NW OF OHIO RIVER, PETITIONERS, ETC. 1790-1800 [1785-1804] (Now Ohio)© Compiled by John D Stemmons, 2021. It contains 217 names for 1790 and 3047 names for 1800. This book may include many heads of household at that time and serves as a substitute for missing or no censuses. It even incorporates the names of many native Americans. These records provide an incredible amount of information about these early people. While censuses help track people, the records this book contains are even better in some respects than the census because it helps us understand some of their personal information not recorded by a census. Some additional biographical details may be included, plus possible relationships with other family members. For information on how to obtain this book search by the title or "Books by John Stemmons" at Amazon.com. This comes automatically with a paperback binding. It includes but is not limited to petitions regarding:

- Petition of the French inhabitants of Gallipolis regarding their purchase of lands from the Scioto Company.
- Inhabitants on the Muskingum to Governor St. Clair.
- Petitions about land and issues with John Cleves Symmes.
- 1800, Population Schedules, Washington County. Territory Northwest of the River Ohio.
- Petition by inhabitants telling of losses in the "Late Indian war" and their inability to obtain land in Kentucky.
- Petition by inhabitants of Hamilton County seeking approval to purchase reserved land in order to build a grist mill because it has a sufficient stream of water.
- List of Gallipolis proprietors and the amount of their land purchases.

285 pages	$57.00

PA-01 PENNSYLVANIA CHESTER COUNTY TAX LIST 1771© Compiled by John D Stemmons, 2021. It contains 5621 names. This record lists all taxable people in the county, and as such, is a good census substitute. It is not known what is meant by the abbreviations or "inmate". Perhaps they were incarcerated in jail or were indentured in some way. Often an occupation is listed. Occasionally there will be information about family relationships. It is helpful that this book includes the information about the taxable property. For information on how to obtain this book search by the title or "Books by John Stemmons" at Amazon.com. This comes automatically with a paperback binding.

399 pages $79.80

South Carolina

South Carolina has a remarkable series of records that makes it unique for the Colonial period. These are the "Jury Lists" compiled by the government to function as a list of names from which members of a jury could be assigned. They cover the period 1720-1783 and, according to the act in 1731, were compiled from tax lists of the preceding year [which no longer exist], listing every person who paid a tax of twenty shillings or more. Those who paid five pounds or more were listed as grand jurors. The poorer class of people would not be listed. While not a complete list of the heads of household, they represent a sizeable proportion. They serve as a census during a period of growth, migration, and war. Usually only the name is given, but sometimes an occupation or name of the father is listed, etc. Many names are on more than one list for a particular year.

1010-**SOUTH CAROLINA 1720 JURY LIST**© Compiled by John D and E. Diane Stemmons, 2004. This publication has 840 entries covering a time when South Carolina was only 50 years old and the population was very small with only an estimated 885 heads of household. Unfortunately, it does not list a residence other than South Carolina. For information on how to obtain this book search by the title or "Books by John Stemmons" at Amazon.com. This comes automatically with a paperback binding.

48 pages $9.60

1017-**SOUTH CAROLINA 1731 JURY LIST**© Compiled by John D and E. Diane Stemmons, 2005. This book contains 2160 entries. It lists the locality of every person. For information on how to obtain this book search by the title or "Books by John Stemmons" at Amazon.com. This comes automatically with a paperback binding.

110 pages $22.00

1011-**SOUTH CAROLINA 1740 JURY LIST**© Compiled by John D and E. Diane Stemmons, 2004. This book contains 2160 entries. It lists the locality of every person. For information on how to obtain this book search by the title or "Books by John Stemmons" at Amazon.com. This comes automatically with a paperback binding.

111 pages $22.20

1012-**SOUTH CAROLINA 1751 JURY LIST**© Compiled by John D and E. Diane Stemmons, 2004. This book contains 2170 entries. It lists the locality of every person. For information on how to obtain this book search by the title or "Books by John Stemmons" at Amazon.com. This comes automatically with a paperback binding.

109 pages $21.80

1013-**SOUTH CAROLINA 1757 JURY LIST**© Compiled by John D and E. Diane Stemmons, 2004. This book contains 2624 entries. It lists the locality of every person. For information on how to obtain this book search by the title or "Books by John Stemmons" at Amazon.com. This comes automatically with a paperback binding.

135 pages $27.00

1014-**SOUTH CAROLINA 1767 JURY LIST**© Compiled by John D and E. Diane Stemmons, 2004. This book contains 2385 entries. It lists the locality of every person. For information on how to obtain this book search by the title or "Books by John Stemmons" at Amazon.com. This comes automatically with a paperback binding.

127 pages $25.40

SC-07 **SOUTH CAROLINA 1780 [1775-1784], VOLUMES 1-2**© Compiled by John D Stemmons, 2021. It contains 13,444 names. This record of jury lists consist of many people during the Colonial/Revolutionary War period and as such, is a good census substitute. Since Loyalists owned property that they paid taxes on, they may be included as well. These records provide a place of residence which can lead to other records to search. For information on how to obtain this book search by the title or "Books by John Stemmons" at Amazon.com. This comes automatically with a paperback binding.

Volume 1, 502 pages $100.40
Volume 2, 575 pages $115.00

TN-01 **TENNESSEE PETITIONS, ETC., 1770-1790 [1765-1794]**© Also known as Territory South of Ohio River. Compiled by John Stemmons, 2021. This book was assembled from *Territorial Papers of the United States* and contains 1 name for 1770, 12 names for 1780, and 1161 names for 1790. These people listed seem to be the more prominent persons, so, most of the less noteworthy individuals would not be listed. Still, the people listed clarify this early time before Tennessee became a state. The amount of biographical information is significant compared to the other books we have compiled from *Territorial Papers of the United States*. Many Native American names are included. For information on how to obtain this book search by the title or "Books by John Stemmons" at Amazon.com. This comes automatically with a paperback binding. It includes but is not limited to petitions regarding:

- "One of twelve men selected by the Cumberland people to govern the settlement, 1783; appointed by the Governor of North Carolina judge of the courts, Davidson County, 1783.
- Appointments about military and local officers, etc.
- Name on the "Treaty of Holston", 2 Jul 1791 between the President of the US and "Chiefs and Warriors of the Cherokee Nation of Indians."
- Memorial, 1 Aug 1791, to the President from the civil and military officers of Mero District explaining recent depredations of the Indians and seeking an "Act of Cession" from North Carolina.

95 pages $19.00

TN-02 **TENNESSEE PETITIONERS, ETC. AND GRAINGER COUNTY TAX LISTS 1800 [1795-1804]**© Compiled by John Stemmons, 2021. Also known as Territory South of Ohio River. This book was assembled from Grainger County Tax Lists 1800 and *Territorial Papers of the United States* and contains 182 names for the *Papers* and 247 names for the tax lists. From *Territorial Papers of the United States* the names mostly seem to be persons appointed to official or military positions or are members of the Knoxville Convention. Thus, they seem to be the more prominent persons, so, most of the less noteworthy individuals would not be listed. Still, the people listed clarify this early time before Tennessee became a state. The tax lists record the names of those who are taxable and are much more inclusive. They do include important details about the property they held. For information on how to obtain this book search by the title or "Books by John Stemmons" at Amazon.com. This comes automatically with a paperback binding. It includes but is not limited to petitions regarding:

- List, 21 Dec 1795, of members of Knoxville Convention.
- Appointments of military and local officers, etc.

49 pages $9.80

TN-03 **TENNESSEE GRAINGER COUNTY TAX LISTS 1810 [1805-1814]**© Compiled by John Stemmons, 2021. This book was assembled from Grainger County Tax Lists 1810 and contains 1242 names of those who are taxable. They do include important details about the property they held and may provide clues regarding

relationship, etc. For information on how to obtain this book search by the title or "Books by John Stemmons" at Amazon.com. This comes automatically with a paperback binding.
146 pages $29.20

TN-04 TENNESSEE GRAINGER COUNTY TAX LISTS 1820 [1815-1824]© Compiled by John Stemmons, 2021. This book was assembled from Grainger County Tax Lists 1820 and contains 1161 names of those who are taxable. They do include important details about the property they held and may provide clues regarding relationship, etc. The lists for 1800-1820 furnish an excellent opportunity to track the population growth of the county. For information on how to obtain this book search by the title or "Books by John Stemmons" at Amazon.com. This comes automatically with a paperback binding.
131 pages $26.20

VA-01 VIRGINIA PERSONAL PROPERTY TAX LISTS, 1780 [1775-1784] (Accomack and Albemarle Counties)© Compiled by John Stemmons, 2021. This book was assembled from Accomack and Albemarle Counties Personal Property Tax Lists ca 1780 and contains 2553 names of those who are taxable. They do include important details about the property they held and may provide clues regarding relationship, etc. They even furnish the entry for, it is assumed, future president Thomas Jefferson! For information on how to obtain this book search by the title or "Books by John Stemmons" at Amazon.com. This comes automatically with a paperback binding.
252 pages $50.40

VA-02 VIRGINIA PERSONAL PROPERTY TAX LISTS, 1790 [1785-1794] (Accomack and Albemarle Counties)© Compiled by John Stemmons, 2021. This book was assembled from Accomack and Albemarle Counties Personal Property Tax Lists ca 1790 and contains

2679 names of those who are taxable, plus 3 from *Territorial Papers of the U.S.* They do include important details about the property they held and may provide clues regarding relationship, etc. They even furnish the entry for, it is assumed, future president Thomas Jefferson! Data on the age range of males is also included. For information on how to obtain this book search by the title or "Books by John Stemmons" at Amazon.com. This comes automatically with a paperback binding.
333 pages $66.60

VA-03 VIRGINIA PERSONAL PROPERTY TAX LISTS, ca 1800 [1795-1804] (Accomack and Albemarle Counties)© Compiled by John Stemmons, 2021. This book was assembled from Accomack and Albemarle Counties Personal Property Tax Lists ca 1800 and contains 3788 names of those who are taxable. They do include important details about the property they held and may provide clues regarding relationship, etc. They even furnish the entry for, it is assumed, future president Thomas Jefferson! Data on the age range of males is also included. With the lists for 1780-1800 one can track population growth in these countries. An individual showing up for the first time may indicate potential age. For information on how to obtain this book search by the title or "Books by John Stemmons" at Amazon.com. This comes automatically with a paperback binding.
436 pages $87.20

Population estimates were obtained from U.S. Bureau of the Census, *Historical Statistics of the United States, Colonial Times to 1957*, Washington, D.C., 1960, Library of Congress Card No. A 60-9150; and United States. Bureau of the Census, *A Century of Population Growth From the First Census of the United States to the Twelfth, 1790-1900* Washington: Government Printing Office, 1909. A household size of 5.7 persons was assumed.

Good morning.
We received the gift book of "Georgia Petitions 1785-1794". Fantastic book and a great tool in researching that time period. I like the format which is easy to read and puts in one place the petitions for research. I personally have searched many of the petitions and love this new tool. The introduction and the list of petitions gives much added information to understanding the petitions for the various individuals.
I look forward to ordering more books in July after our budget is in place. Thank you for contacting our library and making us aware of your fine publications. Have a great day.
Thanks,
Irene Godwin
Ellen Payne Odom Genealogy Library
204 5th St. S.E.
P.O. Box 2828
Moultrie, GA 31768

EXAMPLES OF THE KIND OF INFORMATION CONTAINED IN OUR BOOKS

Cicotte, J. Bte.,   Michigan Territory, District of Detroit, "Cote des Poux"

Cicotte, J. Bte.,	45-Over?	Male	**Color:**	White
10-16		Male	**Color:**	White
10-16		Male	**Color:**	White
16-26		Male	**Color:**	White
45-Over		Female	**Color:**	White

1810 Census of the District of Detroit
MS/Witherell (B. F. H.) Collection, LMS, Burton Historical Collection, Detroit Public Library, Folder 2
Cicotte, Jacques,   Michigan Territory
    Cicotte, Jacques,   Male
Petition, 26 Oct 1807, to Congress from inhabitants of Michigan Ter. seeking time to file claims to their land, claims on 1+ parcels be confirmed, farms on Detroit River be extended to 80 arpents, & occupancy later than 1 Jul 1796 be allowed [pp. 138-49].
Territorial Papers of the US - volume: 10 page: 146
Holeday, Jas,   Territory NW of Ohio River   Knox County, Vincennes
    Holeday, Jas,   Male
Address to Colonel Josiah Harmar by American inhabitants of Post Vincennes dated 4 Aug 1787
Territorial Papers of US - volume: 2 page: 65
Holliday, Heirs of James,   Territory NW of Ohio River   Knox County, Vincennes
    Holliday, Heirs of James,   Male

Petition, 7 Aug 1797, to Congress by inhabitants of Knox County, who migrated to Vincennes around 1786 and received land, but never obtained a deed.
Territorial Papers of US - volume: 2 page: 621
Lajoye, Pierre ,   Spanish North America, St. Louis
     Lajoye, Pierre,   Male
     "Pierre Lajoye, formerly of Prairie du Rocher on the American side of the Mississippi".
Letter, 1790, by Governor St. Clair to Manuel Perez concerning an American boy in the possession of Pierre Lajoye [pages 237-238].
"Mr. Mayet has just complained to me that a Mr. La Joye, to whom he has entrusted an American boy, whom he took from the savages, to be returned to the parents of the latter, has not returned him, but is holding the boy as a slave and refuses to return the boy to them on the pretext of some debt. I am convinced that you will not find it proper that a free child should be held as a slave for the debts of another--and will order Mr. La Joye to return him to Mayet."
Letter, 26 May 1790, from St. Louis by Manuel Perez to Governor St. Clair concerning an American boy in the possession of Pierre Lajoye [pages 237-240]:
"MY DEAR SIR: In order to take cognizance of the subject of the claim in your favor of the 20th instant concerning the child who is today in the possession of Mr. Lajoye, I had the latter appear before me and from the questions which I put to him and the reasons which he advanced to me on this subject I have found in him only a disposition to render service to the Unhappy Father who lost him and who asks for him in a letter of which the said Mr. Lajoye is the bearer.

    After studying this matter carefully, I find that the above-mentioned child claimed by Mr. Mayet can leave the possession of Mr. Lajoye only to go to that of the Father now living at Natches. I think also that it is just for the said Mr. Mayet to be reimbursed for what he actually gave the savages in order to get him out of their barbarous hands; . . .

    When the young man arrived at Mr. Lajoye's house, he came and notified me of it at once and that he would write to the lower part of the Colony to learn in what district the Father of the said child lived. He learned later from the letter of which he is the bearer, that he resides at Natchez; accordingly he will send him down on the first opportunity."
Territorial Papers of the US - volume: 2 page: 237
Mayfield, Geddeon, Kentucky Barren County
     Mayfield, Geddeon,   Male
Acres of land: 200; Barren Co.; watercourse: Mill Creek; Entry: Geddeon Mayfield; Survey: same; Patent: 0; white males over 21: 0; white males 16-21: 0; blacks over 16: 0; total blacks: 0; horses: 0; stud horses: 0; retail stores: 0; tavern license: 0.
Barren County Tax Book, 1800, part 1 - page: 10 FAMILY HISTORY LIBRARY film 7865

LEGISLATIVE PETITIONS

Petitions to the governor, legislature, etc., were a particularly important way for individuals to communicate with their government regarding issues that were very essential to them. Their influence in making changes throughout our history has contributed to making our society what it is today. They are an important link in our legislative and judicial history. In these early petitions one can trace the growing desire for democracy. In fact, they are one of the most visible manifestations of democracy in practice. It is fascinating to view the changes in the reasons for submitting petitions over time (see the lists below.)

Because petitions represent the feelings of one or more individuals, they provide a window into the soul of the petitioners that illuminates the historical landscape. Most aspects of the human condition are addressed in some form by these important documents. The names listed with the petition can be used as a census of inhabitants for a particular locality. Often it is possible to determine useful information about individual persons from these records. They can help compensate for lost or destroyed county records. Petitions are original records that contain historical background about our culture and society.

    Unfortunately, petitions are among the most inaccessible and underused records because there are so many, they are often difficult and time-consuming to read, and are usually housed only in the state archives or other repository in their un-microfilmed condition.

    To help resolve this problem, we have abstracted the content of many petitions and indexed the names of the petitioners. A brief context of the petition is provided with each name. Generally, we have not included those petitions with fewer than 10-12 names.

GENEALOGY AND LOCAL HISTORY BOOKS IN PDF FORMAT ON A FLASH DRIVE

705 Local and Family History books for $75-or 11 cents a book!!! All 4 volumes of Savage's Genealogical Dictionary of New England would cost you about $0.44!*
You can have in your library/home more books of this type than most libraries have. They cover nearly all aspects of human experience including law, medicine, biography, history, etc., etc.

Concerns?
1.   **Question:** I am uncomfortable in letting patrons use this small drive as it may become lost.

Answer: Simply download the contents of the drive onto your computer(s) and keep the drive in a safe place. We will replace it at no charge if it becomes lost.

2. **Question:** Some of our books, including those on microfilm, that are also on your flash drive are in poor condition because of patron use through the years, especially when copies are made. Copies made from microfilm are not always the best quality. How can you help us with these problems?

Answer: Once our books are on your computers, your originals can be kept in a secured area so that no more damage will occur because of hands-on use. The images on the computer can be easily printed, usually with better quality.

3. **Question:** We are only interested in items covering the locality our patrons live in.

Answer: Many of your patrons were born outside of your area and/or have ancestry from all over the United States, etc.

4. **Question:** Are these books under copyright restrictions?

Answer: They are in the public domain and so are not copyrightable.

Approximately how many pages do the 705 books add up to?
Total cost (from Stemmons Publishing) for hard copies: $7044 (not available now)
Approximated total pages of text on the flash drive: 221,307
Approximated total images on the flash drive: 58,272

A huge genealogical library of 705 books on your computer for only $75
A dealer's discount is available of $45 for 5 or more flash drives.
Imagine 705 books… 60,417 images… 230,642 pages on a small flash drive.

You may be able to find these books on Google, Ancestry, or FamilySearch. To make a hard copy from these sources may be expensive, especially if you were to copy all 705! I may be mistaken, but I'm not sure you can print just a single page from those services. You can with my books. You also have them immediately at your fingertips without needing to go to the effort to search these other services.
The downside to these books is that many are not indexed.
No problem: just check the index provided by these other sources before using our books.
"In 2016, popular genealogy blogger Dick Eastman surmised that perhaps ninety percent of the resources you may need to fill out your family tree are not yet available on the Internet." This statement was found on the Boston Public Library website. If that is true, some of the books on our flash drive may not be found on the Internet.

You may obtain a copy of the drive by sending check, money order, or cash to John Stemmons at 1078 Shields Lane, South Jordan, Utah, 801-254-2152 (Call between 9:00 a.m. and 5:00 p.m. Monday through Friday. If no one answers, please leave a message.), stemmonspublishing@gmail.com. We have been in this business since 1975! Check BBB if you need to.

The fee for shipping and handling is $10.00 unless you send a shipping container, deliverable to you, with sufficient postage to mail to you. Please allow 4-6 weeks for delivery.

The books on the drive are in the public domain and are not copyrighted. You may make as many copies of them as you would like. Please do not place the contents of the drive, in part or in full, on the Internet except for individual pages.

We do not do credit cards and PayPal. If you are unhappy with the drive, please return it for a refund of your money.

If you would like a list of questions and answers or a list of the books, please let us know.

*How are we able to do this? Simply by reducing each page so that 2-6 pages can be placed on a single 8½ by 11 sheet of paper and still be readable. With the computer, you can enlarge it as many times as needed.

Number of books by locality:

US-99, Regional-32, AL-1, CT-31, DE-1, GA-2, IL-1, IN-1, KY-1, ME-23, MD-15, MA-91, MI-1, MN-1, MO-2, NH-20, NJ-28, NY-81, NC-9, OH-9, PA-51, RI-6, SC-26, VT-2, VA-47, WV-1; Family History-62; CN-5; EN-39; IR-10; SCOT-7=705 books!

www.ingramcontent.com/pod-product-compliance
Lightning Source LLC
Chambersburg PA
CBHW080245260726
48658CB00008B/3232